4/30

101 Questions and Answers on
the Four Last Things

101 QUESTIONS AND ANSWERS ON THE FOUR LAST THINGS

Joseph T. Kelley

Paulist Press
New York/Mahwah, N.J.

Cover design by Cynthia Dunne
Book design by Theresa M. Sparacio

Library of Congress Cataloging-in-Publication Data

Kelley, Joseph T., 1948–
101 questions and answers on the four last things / Joseph T. Kelley.
   p cm.
   Includes bibliographical references and index.
   ISBN 0-8091-4375-5 (alk. paper)
   1. Eschatology—Miscellanea. 2. Catholic Church—Doctrines—Miscellanea.
I. Title: One hundred and one questions and answers on the last four things.
II. Title: One hundred one questions and answers on the four last things.
III. Title.
BT821.3.K45 2006
236—dc22

                                      2005023195

Published by Paulist Press
997 Macarthur Boulevard
Mahwah, New Jersey 07430

www.paulistpress.com

Printed and bound in the
United States of America

CONTENTS

To my mother and father

ACKNOWLEDGMENTS

My thanks to Dr. Christopher Bellitto of Paulist Press for his invitation to write this book and for his guidance in bringing it to completion. His unfailing combination of encouragement and helpful criticism has made the project both enjoyable and enriching. I also thank my colleagues Dr. Kathleen Fitzpatrick, Joseph Thompson, Orlando Barone, Richard Santagati, James Wenzel, OSA, Kay DeBurro, and Casey Coburn for their encouragement and help in improving the text. The teaching and mentoring of Fr. Charles Curran continue to inform and direct my theological method, and to deepen my ever-growing appreciation of the richness of Catholic theology.

During the year that I was researching and writing this text, a former teacher and dear friend, Sr. Rose Frangione, IHM, suffered through her difficult, final illness and entered into the glory of the risen Lord and the life of the Trinity. Her deep faith and courageous witness were with me throughout this endeavor.

Finally, I am grateful for the support and patience of my wife Alina, my children Kasia and Patyrk, and also of my parents, whose long lives have been a special blessing for our whole family. My Augustinian brothers and sisters remain my beloved companions and fellow pilgrims.

Joseph T. Kelley

A NOTE ON SCRIPTURAL CITATIONS

Christian thinking and teaching about death, judgment, hell, and heaven depend to a very great extent on what the Bible—both the Hebrew scriptures (commonly called the Old Testament by Christians) and the New Testament—have to say about these topics. So the Bible is cited liberally throughout this text.

For those not familiar with how biblical citations are noted, the following may be helpful. When a particular passage from scripture is quoted or cited as relevant, the name of the biblical book is given, followed by the chapter, and then after a colon the verse or verses. Thus **Exod 24:3** means the Book of Exodus, chapter 24, verse 3. **2 Cor 2:3–10, 15** means the Second Letter to the Corinthians, chapter 2, verses 3 to 10 and also verse 15. A semicolon closes the chapter being cited and opens a new chapter. Thus **Exod 19:18; 33:9** means the Book of Exodus, chapter 19, verse 18; and chapter 33, verse 9. I use the commonly accepted abbreviations for the names of biblical books.

The reader is encouraged to refer to the biblical passages cited for a deeper understanding of the origins of the theological ideas presented here.

INTRODUCTION

For now we see in a mirror, dimly....
—1 Corinthians 13:12

There are many reasons you may have picked up this book. Perhaps you recently lost a loved one. You may hope to find here some answers to the hundred and one questions that death delivers. Or perhaps you hope to answer the one painful question that recurs in your grief a hundred times every day. Where is he now? Can she remember me? Will we meet again? Is there really life and happiness after death? You may be working through such haunting questions and painful feelings with the support of others in a bereavement group. Or you may be taking a more academic approach to these ultimate questions in a class on death and dying.

Some readers may themselves have had their own brush with death through a serious illness or a bad accident. They will bring their own unique memories and insights to the questions posed here. For them death is no longer an abstract philosophical question, but a foe personally faced, a threat already met. Some who open these pages may have had the experience of being considered clinically dead and then resuscitated. Their near-death experience certainly provides a lens through which they will view the ideas presented here.

Whatever our different personal experiences with death, it is the one event in which we all eventually share. We cannot but have certain feelings about the end of our life on this Earth and what

1

may lie beyond. When our own mortality begins to loom large, thoughts of death can preoccupy us, depress us, and frighten us through the long loneliness of a sleepless night. Our fear may be tinged with doubt, or even despair. Might death be just dissolution into nothingness? Will my death be the end of me? A thousand and one questions could not begin to address the diversity of experience, belief, and feeling brought to such a topic as this.

Besides the certainty of our own individual end and the uncertainty of what lies beyond, there are also questions about the destiny of the human race in the design of the universe and about the fate of our planet amid the company of stars and galaxies. We search among the religions of the world; we read through the thoughts of sages; we compare the theories of science for any hints or insights that might give us some certitude or hope about ultimate questions and answers. We also wonder, both as individuals and as communities of belief, about moral or karmic connections between the choices we make from day to day and the final state of our souls.

The answers in this little book present the long tradition of Christian thought about ultimate matters. Christian teachings, and specifically the Catholic formulation of those teachings, inform the reflections offered here on the subjects of death, of judgment after death, of possible states of existence in the afterlife, and of the final end of humanity and creation. That faith not only offers some answers, but also provides the words and concepts that help form the questions as well. So both the questions and the answers offered here reveal the way one community of religious faith goes about reflecting on the last things.

Christians believe in a loving God who revealed the depths of the divine mystery in the person and preaching of the first-century Galilean rabbi, Jesus of Nazareth. In Jesus, according to Christian creed, the Holy and Eternal One entered into human history and joined in human destiny. Jesus shared both our life and our death. Christians believe that God raised Jesus from the dead and thereby conquered death for all of us. By God's loving grace and the gift of the Holy Spirit, we share in Jesus' victory over death and will enjoy his risen life with the Father. All humanity, indeed all creation, was made to share in the eternal life of God at the end of time and the final consummation of all things.

These beliefs guide Christians through their wondering about ultimate matters. The context, creed, and conviction of their faith set parameters for the way Christians pose questions about death and the afterlife and on the way they formulate their answers. We will follow that way of faith here. We will trace the ancient path that committed and thoughtful Christian thinkers have explored over centuries and millennia of reflection on the promise of eternal life.

A sustained and disciplined reflection on human experience in light of faith is called "theology." Theology is faith in action on an intellectual level. It is motivated by the passion to apply all the resources of human reason and experience in an always restless search for deeper understandings of and insights into the teachings of one's religious tradition. When we turn our attention to questions about death and the afterlife, our theological reflection is called "eschatology." This somewhat formidable term comes from the Greek word *eschaton,* which means "end" or "goal." Eschatology is the theological study of the end of time, both the end and goal of our individual time here on Earth, and the end and goal of time itself.

Although founded on faith in what God has revealed, theology is nonetheless a limited human endeavor. As we scan the horizons of human thought, explore the frontiers of faith, and peer into the eternal beyond, we must do so with humility. When speaking, thinking, and writing about God and God's final purpose for us, we must remember that our language is limited, our concepts provisional, and our perspective narrow. The categories and experiences of our present life are all we have to anticipate or interpret the life to come and its Author. We cannot know God directly, at least not now. Our knowledge of God, and of what God has prepared for us, is imperfect. "For now we see in a mirror, dimly, but then we will see face to face. Now I know only in part; then I will know fully, even as I have been fully known" (1 Cor 13:12).

What the church teaches about death, judgment, hell, and heaven is expressed in the language of symbol, of image, of incomplete and imperfect representation. Through faith we can see only the dim outlines of what may lie ahead for us. When posing questions about and formulating answers on such topics, it is tempting to fall into a kind of surety and literalism that is very seductive. We can quickly become fundamentalists about the four last things, shooting back nicely formulated and neatly formatted responses that we quickly forget are only very weak, preliminary precursors to the realities.

Death and the afterlife, like the God they intimate, are far beyond human dictate. In theology they are called "mysteries of faith." The word *mystery* has two different connotations. First there is the mystery of a difficult puzzle or an unsolved crime. Some of the pieces of a puzzle are perplexing; some facts about a crime are unknown. A clever puzzle master will put the pieces together and bring the whole picture to resolution. Or, faced with an uncertain scenario, a dogged detective will slowly uncover all the clues and solve the crime. This kind of mystery, of a puzzle or a crime, is ultimately solvable. The mysterious dissolves with the necessary and sufficient knowledge, and the persistence to gain it.

There is a second way, however, of understanding mystery. *Mystery* can also describe something that is never solvable, never complete, never closed. For example, when you find that someone loves you unconditionally and without reserve, you are confronted with a reality that you can never fully penetrate, exhaust, or explain. To love fully and to be loved totally is an ever-growing, changing, and challenging mystery that confronts us with its continually unfolding nature. Likewise, when you experience a painting or sculpture or musical composition that invites you into its reality again and again in an inexhaustible combination of thought and emotion and desire that change who you are and how you live—that's also a mystery of this second type. The ecstasies of love and aesthetics are mysteries that we enter, not solve; that we receive, not resolve; that we abide in, not foreclose.

Indeed, the human mysteries of love and beauty are perhaps among the best of theological analogies or ways into the mystery that is God and into a careful reflection on what God has prepared for us. Christian faith invites us to think of God as infinite love, endless beauty, constantly inviting us into relationship, seeking our acceptance and engagement, challenging and changing us at every level of our being. It is the task of theology to reflect carefully, lovingly, endlessly on the divine mystery and on the startling revelation that infinite love seeks to draw us into its endless loveliness. When theology turns its attention to death and the afterlife, it is really asking about the end, the goal, the final purpose of divine love itself.

It is toward, in and for love, the divine love, that our hundred and one questions about the four last things move along from one to the next. The questions and answers in these pages are as so many steps on a pilgrimage of love: love for those who have preceded us in life and death, love for our present traveling companions, and love for those who will certainly follow us along this same way of questioning and struggling for answers. For "the Love that moves the sun and the other stars" (*Divine Comedy, Paradiso,* Canto XXXIII, 145) is the very same love that helps us make this theological journey toward the One who is the source of all love and loveliness.

1. Why four last things?

The four last things—death, judgment, heaven, and hell—first appear as a quartet in the theological books of the twelfth and thirteenth centuries. When Christian theologians of the Middle Ages such as Peter Abelard and Saint Thomas Aquinas wrote about death and about the end of the world, they saw these four faith realities as the only things left. At the moment of individual death the believer leaves behind church, sacraments, doctrine, scripture, even faith and morals. Only the four last things remain. Likewise, at the end of the world all theological distinctions and categories will have served their purpose and will be dispensed with—except these four last things.

A few hundred years later, in the sixteenth and seventeenth centuries, both Catholic and Protestant preachers employed the four last things in their sermons and teachings for the spiritual welfare of individual Christian believers, to prepare them for the end. Lent and other penitential occasions were popular venues for these sobering themes. Even well into the twentieth century, Christian congregations and devout souls were regularly treated to dour doses of the four last things.

The Second Vatican Council (1962–1965) encouraged Christians to return to biblical texts and to writings from the early centuries of the church. So theologians studied what the Hebrew scriptures (the Old Testament), and the Christian New Testament had to say about ultimate things. They also took another look at early Christian writers on these themes. What has emerged is a new appreciation of the kingdom of God, the doctrine of the resurrection, and God's renewal and completion of all creation at the end of time. Encouraged by Vatican II, Catholics and other Christians have renewed their appreciation of these important themes in the teachings of Jesus and in the faith of the early centuries of the church. Today when preachers and teachers turn our attention to final and ultimate things, they are more likely to call us to reflect on the fulfillment of faith, hope, and love rather than on impending doom and destruction. We follow their lead here in this book.

ONE

DEATH

Death in Scripture and Theology

2. How is death understood in the Hebrew scriptures?

There is no one, systematic understanding of death in the Hebrew scriptures. In general, however, the Hebrews were pessimistic and fatalistic about death. They believed that death meant the end of one's relationship with God.

This sounds strange to us today. We presume that death is the door through which we go to meet God. The Hebrews, however, understood their relationship with God to be mediated through God's covenant with them as a people here on this Earth. They each enjoyed God's love and favor because they were all members of the one and only nation chosen by God. Relationship with God was mediated through the clan and tribe. Death meant final separation from that extended family of faith and worship. So it also meant separation from God.

Death was not, however, extinction or annihilation of the person. Borrowing from the mythology of their Canaanite and Mesopotamian neighbors, the Hebrews imagined a dark, shadowy underworld that received all who died, regardless of their rank or station in life, and irrespective of how well or badly they had lived. They called this underworld *sheol*. Once in *sheol* a person was beyond God's covenant with Israel. The author of Psalm 88 prays that current troubles not lead to death and separation from God: "Is your steadfast love declared in the grave...? Are your wonders known in the darkness, or your saving help in the land of forgetfulness?" (vv. 11,13). The presumed answer to all these questions is no. Many scriptural passages give poignant expression to the depths of human dread and anxiety in the face of death. (See, for example, Ps 30 and Isa 38.) The most troubling part of

11

death for the devout psalmist is that it leaves one outside the span of God's attention (question 63).

In the later books of the Hebrew scriptures, amid moral dilemmas about good people who suffer (as in the story of Job), and with the rise of apocalyptic writings (such as the Book of Daniel), scattered hints and glimmers of hope about some kind of afterlife begin to appear. Question 10 deals with these later developments in Hebrew thought.

3. How is death understood in the Christian New Testament?

In contrast to the Hebrew scriptures, the New Testament is unequivocally optimistic about death. "Death has been swallowed up in victory. Where, O Death, is your victory? Where, O Death, is your sting?" (1 Cor 15:54–55). For the early Christians, Jesus' death changed everything, because on the cross God suffered the final human fate and conquered it. Death is no longer a one-way trip to *sheol* and separation from God. In the person of Jesus, divinity itself joined humankind and entered into the mystery of death and dying.

4. How does the New Testament interpret Jesus' death?

In the New Testament, Christ's death is described as "sacrificial," as "redemptive," and as a "return" to the Father.

To *sacrifice* something is to set it aside for God, to separate it from its ordinary use or usual place in order that it might honor the Creator. Since Jesus died during Passover, his followers associated his crucifixion with the Passover sacrifice. His death was like the sacrifice of the paschal lamb by which the Jews remembered their escape from Egypt and slavery. Jesus' death frees us from slavery to sin and opens the way through death into a new life in God.

Jesus' death is also *redemptive*. In Hebrew tradition a redeemer (*goel*) was the person appointed to secure the release and return of kidnapped relatives. By offering gold or goods or even himself, a redeemer's mission was to bring the captives home. The New Testament speaks often of Jesus securing our redemption (Rom 2:24; Eph 1:7,14; Heb 9:12). He sacrifices himself to secure the release of all the captives of *sheol* who had led good lives and to bring them back to God (question 66).

Jesus' death is also a *return*. John's Gospel emphasizes that Jesus was himself the divine Word of God. His death was a going back to the Father from whom he had come (John 8:23,58; 17:5,18,24; 18:37). So when we die he becomes our way into the divine mystery and eternal life. Jesus' death means that death itself is transformed from a dead end into a new beginning.

From the second to the seventh centuries, Christian writers known as the "Fathers of the Church," continued and expanded on these three ways of interpreting the meaning of Jesus' death, laying the foundation for subsequent centuries of Christian theology.

5. Did Jesus really die?

This is a question that we can trace back to the very beginning of Christianity. The Gospels assert quite clearly that Jesus died on the cross. "But when they came to Jesus and saw that he was already dead, they did not break his legs" (John 19:33). Within the first century or two of Christianity, however, some believers began to deny that Jesus actually died. They reasoned that if Jesus is truly God, and if God is incapable of suffering and death, then Jesus did not really suffer or die.

Such ideas were popular among certain sects of believers called "Gnostics," who claimed to have a secret, spiritual knowledge that would save them. They also believed the material world, including the human body, was the work of the devil. One Gnostic sect, called the "Sabellians," after the second-century priest Sabellius, taught that the crucifixion was actually a masquerade and that Jesus never suffered or died.

The church as a whole, however, rejected such thinking. Early summaries of basic Christian teachings, called "creeds" or "professions of faith," refer explicitly to Jesus' death as an article of faith.

6. What has the church taught about death over the centuries?

The church's teachings about death fall into three categories: sacramental, pastoral, and ethical. The New Testament authors, especially Saint Paul, affirm that by the waters of baptism a believer enters into the mystery of Christ's death. In its practice of baptizing new members, the church continues to proclaim the good news that in Jesus the unfathomable mystery of divine, infinite love dwells in the depths of human living and invades the darkness of human dying. Through baptism we enter into the sacrificial death of Christ that is the revelation and the reality of that outpouring of divine love. Baptized Christians remember the abiding reality of Jesus' death, and their mystical participation in it, each time they celebrate the sacrament of the Eucharist. So the two *sacraments* of baptism and Eucharist are the church's main ways of being united with the redemptive death of Jesus.

Pastorally, the church strives to help its members approach their own deaths with the awareness and conviction of faith, and with the comfort and strength of the Eucharist. When a dying person is able to take holy communion, it is called *viaticum,* a word that comes from the two Latin words, *via tecum,* meaning "to take it along with you." As part of the last rites, dying Christians take the eucharistic Christ into the moment and mystery of their own death. Two other sacraments, the anointing of the sick and reconciliation, can also be part of the last rites.

Ethically, the church has taught that death, like life, is sacred. No one should take the life of another—except when absolutely necessary in self-defense. We are also called to respect our own life and death: suicide is not permitted. But neither is it necessary to take extraordinary means to prolong life. Death is a natural part of life, and people of faith can accept it with hope born of faith.

A final point: The church has always held martyrs in special honor. Martyrs choose death at the hands of a persecutor rather than deny their faith in Christ. In their deaths they participate in a special way in the sacrificial nature of Christ's death on the cross.

7. What about near-death experiences?

Let's review some medical distinctions, specifically clinical death, brain death, and biological death. *Clinical death* occurs when all external signs of life are gone: when someone is not breathing, has no pulse, and is unconscious. As paradoxical as it sounds, clinical death is not always fatal. Vital functions and eventually consciousness can sometimes be restored by CPR after a drowning or heart attack, or by surgery to relieve the pressure in a traumatized skull, or by antidotes to poisons and drug overdoses.

At a certain point, however, clinical death resolves into brain death. *Brain death* is the irreversible cessation of all brain function, including the brain stem, due to a sustained lack of blood circulation. In medical terms, no one has ever been revived after brain death. Without extraordinary means to keep the heart and lungs working, brain death will result very quickly in *biological death,* which is the irreversible disintegration of life at the cellular level and the collapse of the intricately interdependent systems of the body.

People who report near-death experiences are those who have been revived after clinical death. What they report may have something to teach us about death itself as a human experience, or at least about the beginning of the death experience. Yet we cannot be sure of that, since they have not suffered brain death or biological death. The church has issued no explicit teaching on this matter.

8. At what point does the soul leave the body?

There is no definite teaching on this question either. Given our current medical knowledge, however, we could suggest that this moment just precedes or coincides somehow with brain death. Yet we cannot be certain. It is important to remember that the Christian understanding of death is a theological reflection, and not a medical or legal definition.

9. What about ghosts?

There are certainly scriptural texts that mention ghosts. The ghost of Samuel arises from *sheol* to admonish Saul (1 Sam 28:11ff). In Jesus' story about the impoverished Lazarus, the deceased rich man asks God if he can return from the dead to warn his equally uncaring brothers to repent (Luke 16:20–31). Upon seeing Jesus moving across the Sea of Galilee, the disciples fear it is a ghost (Matt 14:26). In the postresurrection narratives, Jesus assures the disciples he is no disembodied spirit, but their beloved teacher raised from the dead (Luke 24:36–44; John 20:20,27; 21:5,12).

The ancient Hebrews, the early Christians, and most cultures up until the time of the Enlightenment in the seventeenth and eighteenth centuries took for granted the existence of spirits of the dead who might indeed upon occasion visit the land of the living. Even today many indigenous cultures share that assumption. Catholic tradition allows for visions that may involve the souls of deceased saints or loved ones. However, it takes a somewhat cautious approach to such claims and prefers to reflect on the nature of the afterlife in terms of the communion of saints, and of purgatory, heaven, and hell—all of which we will address later in this book.

Visions of the Blessed Virgin or of Christ himself do not fit into the category of "ghosts," for both Jesus and Mary have been raised, body and soul, according to Catholic teaching, Jesus in his resurrection and Mary in her assumption (question 90). So let's turn now to the meaning of resurrection.

Resurrection from the Dead

10. Is resurrection mentioned in the Hebrew scriptures?

The Hebrew scriptures are concerned primarily with the conviction that God chose Israel from all the nations of the Earth. Their focus is on this life and how to live well in this world as God's chosen people. The afterlife is an afterthought.

In two psalms we find a growing hope, however, that the covenant that Israel enjoys with God will never end. Psalms 49 and 73 proclaim that God will be with the psalmist even in death, and that only outright rebellion against the covenant could break one's relationship with God. Still, this hope does not resolve into any sustained claims about afterlife.

It is only with the rise of a new kind of Hebrew literature, called "apocalyptic," that affirmations of an afterlife erupt into the scriptures.

11. What are apocalyptic writings?

Apocalyptic writings appear during the persecution of the Jews by the Syrian Greeks around 300 BCE. Among the colorful imagery and defiant protests of apocalyptic writings, we find proclamations of eventual victory over the occupying political power and the establishment of God's reign in Israel and throughout the world. Isaiah 16:41 and 26:19 and Daniel 12:2–3 promise that the faithful who have died will return and share in the victory of God's kingdom. Such faith in an eternal victory for the just also resolves Job's dilemma about the good who know only suffering in this life.

The books of the Hebrew scriptures that are heavily influenced by the apocalyptic movement include Ezekiel, Daniel, and various passages in Isaiah. Many other Jewish apocalyptic writings were not included among the official books of the Hebrew scriptures. They remained very influential, however, in developing Jewish thought and culture and in shaping New Testament categories and ideas.

12. Besides apocalyptic literature, are there other books among the Hebrew scriptures that affirm a life after death?

The Book of Wisdom, written in Alexandria, Egypt, around 100 BCE, also affirms life after death (Wis 34:6). Wisdom makes the distinction between body and soul—a distinction foreign to ancient Hebrew language, belief, and culture—and affirms the survival of the soul after death, as Socrates had. The Book of Wisdom, however, was not accepted by the rabbis in Jerusalem because it was written in Greek, not Hebrew, and sounded too much like Greek philosophy. Nonetheless, it did influence the development of Jewish eschatology and further strengthened belief in the survival and eternal happiness of each individual believer.

By the end of the Old Testament period, some groups within Israel embraced the apocalyptic promise of the resurrection of the just to eternal life. However, they would have understood such a return from the dead to involve the whole person, not just an immaterial soul. The Pharisees mentioned in the New Testament were a Jewish sect that cherished apocalyptic hopes and believed in the resurrection of the body. The Sadducee party, however, rejected both (Acts 23:6–9). Even today there is disagreement among believing Jews about the possibility and nature of an afterlife.

13. What does the New Testament mean by Jesus' resurrection from the dead?

The New Testament proclaims and interprets Jesus' resurrection from the dead in light of three themes from the Hebrew scriptures: the kingdom of God, God's covenant with Israel, and, God's ongoing creation.

Jesus began his preaching with the refrain, "The time is fulfilled, and the *kingdom* of God has come near" (Mark 1:15). Such language stirred the hearts of his Jewish listeners with apocalyptic hopes and promises. The kingdom or reign of God meant that God's presence and power would permeate all of creation and society, would oust evil and heal those who suffered from it, and would establish peace and justice everywhere (question 83). Jesus' miracles are the first evidence that God's reign was beginning, as illness, evil, and injustice fall before him. The resurrection is the climax of all these miracles, a complete incursion of divine presence and power in the world, the inauguration of the kingdom, and the end of the ages.

Jesus' resurrection is also the fulfillment of God's *covenant* with Israel. In Jesus' life and death, God seals forever the ancient covenant first offered to Abraham and his descendants and then through Moses to the Hebrews. By raising Jesus from the dead, the Father affirms that nothing, not even death, can negate the fierce bonds of divine love. The resurrection of Jesus reveals the infinite passion of God's covenant love and proclaims that it is extended to all humankind.

Finally, Jesus' resurrection from the dead is a continuation and fulfillment of *creation* itself. All creation came to be through the divine Word. "In the beginning was the Word....All things came into being through him, and without him not one thing came into being" (John 1:1,3). Jesus' resurrection is the beginning of the final act of divine creation, for in the resurrection all created reality is reunited with the divine Word who first called it into being. All things come together and reach their created fullness in the mystery of the risen Christ (Col 1:15–20).

Christ's resurrection is the fullest revelation of God's power *(kingdom),* love *(covenant),* and purpose *(creation).*

14. How did the apostles know that Jesus rose from the dead?

The New Testament is clear about this. Some of Jesus' followers who were with him during his earthly ministry—just how many we don't know—are called in the New Testament "witnesses" to the risen Christ (1 Cor 15:5–8; 1 Thess 2:13). They did not observe Jesus emerging physically from his tomb—no one did. Rather, they had several profound experiences of Jesus alive, transformed, and glorified after his death.

This was not only a deeply interior, subjective, religious experience. It was also an objective experience because their encounters with Christ changed them, their lives, their relationships, and their understanding of God's plan. All of what are called the "postresurrection narratives" in the Gospels are attempts by the New Testament authors to reflect on, interpret, and proclaim to the whole Christian community the power and meaning of these encounters with the risen Lord that radically changed those first witnesses.

15. Wasn't the empty tomb proof of Jesus' resurrection?

The New Testament proclamation of the resurrection is based on the witness of the disciples mentioned in the answer to question 14. The stories about the women finding an empty tomb and angels (Matt 28; Mark 16; Luke 24), about Mary Magdalene's meeting Jesus and mistaking him at first for the gardener (John 20:11–18), about Jesus appearing to the apostles first in Jerusalem and then in Galilee (Matt 28:7,10,16; Luke 24:50; John 20; 21): all of these postresurrection stories are theological meditations on the profound meaning of Jesus' victory over death as experienced by those first witnesses.

Some scholars argue that it does not really matter whether the tomb was empty or not, so powerful was the disciples' experience of the risen Lord. Others would argue that a Jewish understanding of the unity of the person (questions 12 and 21) required an empty tomb. They would also hold that faith in Jesus' resurrection would have been contradicted and discouraged if Jesus' body were found decaying in its tomb.

It is clear in the New Testament that Christian faith in the risen Lord is not based primarily on an empty tomb, but on those first disciples who witnessed him alive and glorified. When Mary Magdalene returns to the apostles, she reports not that the tomb was empty, but that she had "seen the Lord" (John 20:18). When the two disciples, who had met and dined with Jesus on the road to Emmaus on Easter Sunday evening, reported their experience to the apostles gathered in Jerusalem, the response was, "The Lord has risen indeed, and he has appeared to Simon" (Luke 24:34). The heart of resurrection faith is this experience, this seeing the risen Lord.

16. What does resurrection from the dead mean for the rest of us?

Jesus' resurrection is redemptive for us. It was not a solitary, isolated event that happened to Jesus a long time ago, affecting him alone, prefiguring a parallel event that will happen to us some day. His death and resurrection is an eternally present event that we share in here and now. By baptism we are *already* immersed into the mystery of Jesus' victory over death, and we *already* share in his union with the Father.

So we do not have to die physically in order to be part of the new life of the risen Christ. By faith and baptism our humanity, our person, our very self is already being transformed by the power of Christ's resurrection. This is what Paul refers to when he writes, "For you have died, and your life is hidden with Christ in God" (Col 3:3).

When our time on Earth comes to an end, our death becomes the occasion of entering ever more deeply into the mystery of the resurrection. We will cross into eternal union with the Father and the Spirit, "where Jesus, a forerunner on our behalf, has entered..." (Heb 6:20). At the final resurrection of the dead, all humanity and all creation will be transformed and united with God through Christ.

17. Is that why the funeral mass is now called "the mass of the resurrection"?

Yes. When a Catholic dies, the church community gathers to celebrate the mystery of Christ's death and resurrection in the liturgy of the Eucharist. The deceased was once baptized into Christ, and now through death has entered ever more deeply into the mystery of Christ's resurrection. So the funeral liturgy is both a renewal of faith for the participants and a comfort for the bereaved. In the celebration of the Eucharist, the living are actually united through Christ with their loved one who has passed on.

18. Are there other prayers or rituals for the deceased?

There are prayers and scripture readings suggested for those gathered around the deathbed. There is also a liturgical service of scriptural readings and prayers for the wake, or "vigil" as it is properly called. According to local custom, the rosary or other common prayers can also be recited together before or after the vigil service. After the funeral mass of the resurrection, there is a service of committal of the body at the gravesite.

In some circumstances, depending on the local custom or pastoral need, the funeral may be a simpler service of the word in the home or at the cemetery without a celebration of the Eucharist. In all these variations, it is the resurrection of Christ and the hope it inspires that is remembered and celebrated.

19. What about cremation?

For many years, the church strongly discouraged the practice of cremation but did not actually forbid it. You can understand this hesitation about cremation when you consider the importance of the resurrection of the body in Christian faith. Christian tradition and liturgy have always honored the remains of the deceased because of belief in bodily resurrection and in anticipation of that mystery.

In many countries, however, space for burial is limited. So for pastoral reasons, since 1983, canon (church) law has acknowledged cremation as an option, so long as it is not done for reasons that deny Christian teaching. Liturgical directions for cremation were provided in 1997. The ritual encourages that cremation be done after the mass of resurrection. If the body is cremated before the funeral, the remains are treated with dignity and respect and can be brought to the church for the mass of resurrection. There should be no religious service at the actual place of cremation. The remains are to be buried or entombed in a mausoleum with the service of committal. They should not be spread into the air or water.

20. What is the final resurrection from the dead?

The apocalyptic writings of the New Testament emerged during the persecutions of Christians by the Roman Empire. Like Jewish apocalyptic literature, which was their wider context, Christian apocalyptic passages point toward an end of history as we know it. We find prophecy about the end of time in various places, such as Matthew 24 and 25, Mark 13, Paul's two Letters to the Thessalonians, and the whole Book of Revelation. These passages tell us that Christ will return and establish the fullness of the kingdom of God, that he will judge all humanity, and that all the just who have died will share forever in the glory of the risen and victorious Christ. This victory of the just will be the final resurrection of the dead.

We can reflect on the final resurrection of the dead in light of the teaching of creation. We usually think of creation as something that happened fifteen billion years ago or so, when the Big Bang exploded the universe into being. A biblical understanding, however, sees creation as continuous. God sustains creation and moves it along through time and space toward a fulfillment and completion that we do not yet comprehend and can hardly imagine. The final resurrection of the dead means that we humans are destined to be part of the fulfillment and completion of creation. The God who created us through our parents and who sustains us every moment of our existence is also fashioning our participation in that final time. Christ's resurrection is God's pledge that the eternal Word who brought all things into being will restore us, together with all of creation, to the fullness of our being in God.

21. Where will my soul be after I die and before the final resurrection from the dead?

This is a difficult question, for two reasons. First of all, the notion of a soul that survives the death of the body is a Greek idea. The Greek philosophers who believed in human immortality understood it to be only a spiritual survival of the person's soul. Being reunited with one's body was not an attractive idea to the Greeks, who considered matter inferior to spirit, and who considered death a final liberation from the physical world. Resurrection of the body is an apocalyptic Hebrew belief, affirmed and extended by the early Christians. It understands our final end eventually to incorporate our total being, including our physical, spiritual, moral, intellectual, and relational selves.

This is a difficult question also because it presumes that our categories of time and arbitrary units of clock and calendar can be applied to the afterlife. Time is a category or construction of human consciousness. We can use it to imagine what life after death might be like, but we should do so cautiously, with the awareness that it may apply only in a limited way, if at all.

So really, all we can say in response to this question is that our sharing in the unending covenant love of the risen Christ is intensified when we die and enter into the mystery of God. It will not, however, be completed and fulfilled until all of creation is renewed and reunited with Christ. This apocalyptic end time will involve the transformation of all physical creation. As human beings our personal experience of, and our sharing in, physical creation is through our bodies. The final resurrection will somehow complete us because it will involve a final transformation and reunification of all created reality, including what you and I and all human beings have experienced in and through and with our physical bodies.

Survival of the Person

22. Will I still be me after I die?

Yes. In Christian teaching the integrity of the individual survives death, for every person is unique and precious in God's love. How we experience our individuality after death, however, might be very different from our experience of being a separate self in this life.

Think of how our sense of self develops over the many years of human growth. The newborn infant's sense of self is very much bound up with the self of the mother or primary caregiver. As the child grows, she or he gradually establishes more and more of a sense of separateness. Our sense of self continues to grow as we psychologically mature.

What's more, the human experience of being a separate individual varies quite a bit from culture to culture. In the industrialized Western world, we prize our individuality and independence very much. In many cultures of the East and of the Southern hemisphere, a sense of group belonging and shared identity is more important. So if even in this life our sense of "being me" can vary from one phase of life to another, and from one culture to another, we could expect that our sense of self, of "being me," could be radically different in the afterlife.

The real question here is this: How will I experience my individual sense of self when I enter and dwell in the mystery of the eternal, infinite, loving God from whom I have received my very being? It could be a very different experience. The scriptures attest both to change and to continuity between our earthly self and what is to follow. "So it is with the resurrection of the dead. What is sown is perishable, what is raised is imperishable. It is sown in dishonor, it is raised in glory. It is sown in weakness, it is raised in power. It is sown a physical body, it is raised a spiritual body. If there is a physical body, there is also a spiritual body" (1 Cor 15:42–44). (See questions 88, 89.)

23. Will I still have my memories?

Memory is a basic ingredient in our experience of being human. It is the very context of human self-consciousness and of being a person. The great tragedy of an illness such as Alzheimer's disease is that a person loses his or her memories and the capacity to retain and sustain memory. Memory is the glue of human consciousness. Without our capacity to remember, our sense of self begins to disintegrate. For the ancient Hebrews the worst thing about the land of *sheol* was its lack of memory: the dead forgot who they were, and God forgot about them.

So it seems that Christian belief in the survival of the person after death includes the survival of memory. Unless there were to be total discontinuity between the being I am now and what I am to be after my death, memory must somehow be a dimension of that new life. However, the way by which all the events of my life on this Earth are remembered or reappropriated after death may be very different from how memory functions in this life on Earth.

As with our sense of self, so the role of memory and the power of remembered events and relationships vary quite a bit even in this life. The brain must mature to a certain point for the child to be able to process and retain memories. Often what we call "memories" from our earliest years are more likely our creative reconstruction of events reported to us by others, enriched with our own sentiments, and embellished by our later capacities for narrative and connection.

Furthermore, what about all those things that have happened throughout our lives that are buried in our unconscious, lost in the fog of the forgotten? Events reinforced by strong feelings of joy or fear or sorrow at the time they happened are easier to recall, and sometimes hard to forget. When we do recall them time after time, our memory itself layers the event with multiple levels of feelings and stratums of interpretation.

So even in this life, memory is among the most complex and mysterious of human realities. Memory is intricately intertwined with the categories of time and space that define our human experience. If death is somehow an entrance into eternity, it would seem that time and space may give way to wider realities. Yet it also seems reasonable to assume that the continuity of the person before and after death requires a link that must be somehow similar to what we call "memory."

24. Can we believe in reincarnation?

In honoring the sanctity of each person, Christian theology and Catholic teaching have consistently opposed the idea of reincarnation. Christian thought takes history seriously. Our very experience of self is rooted in and to some extent defined by the particular time, place, and culture we inhabit. We encounter God and grace through these humble contingencies of our lives. We respond to the circumstances of our lives and make decisions that help shape our destinies. God respects our choices and honors the uniqueness of each human life.

Death is the final act that seals our decisions and confirms our choices. Christianity teaches that upon death we enter eternally into God's presence—or not, depending on how we have responded to God's overtures of love and grace during our lives. We do not return again and again to live out another human life, but arrive in God to live and enjoy the divine beauty and love forever.

25. Will I meet my loved ones and friends who have died before me?

In their creeds Christians affirm their belief in "the communion of saints." This communion is a mystical relationship among the faithful on this Earth, in purgatory (questions 37–44), and in heaven (questions 81–87).

So, yes, relationship is an important, indeed a key dimension of life after death. We can expect to share eternal life with our loved ones. Like our sense of self and our memories, however, our relationships change and grow throughout life. So, too, the nature of our relationships in the life to come may be different from the ways we relate to each other in this life.

There are two important Christian teachings that give a glimpse of the nature of relationships in eternal life. One is the Christian teaching of love. If the very nature of God is love, and if our human love is already a sharing in God's life (1 John 4:16), then love must be the foundation for our shared life in God after death. How love itself will be transformed by the immediate presence of the eternal, loving One, we do not know. "Beloved, we are God's children now; what we will be has not yet been revealed. What we do know is this: when he is revealed, we will be like him, for we will see him as he is" (1 John 3:2).

A second Christian teaching about relationships in the afterlife is that they will not be exclusive. "For in the resurrection they neither marry nor are given in marriage, but are like angels in heaven" (Matt 22:30). In this life our capacity for deep, abiding, and focused love is limited. Limited time, energy, and responsibility shape the ways in which we give and receive love in this life. If we are married, we dedicate the majority of our personal and spiritual resources to our spouse. If we have children, they require more and more of us. Friends, colleagues, and relatives who form the inner circle of our relationships command our commitment and draw on our reserves. It is a challenge to balance all the competing demands of love.

According to Jesus' words, the limitations of time and space, of verve and vitality inherent in this life do not apply in the life to come. Eternal love will be limitless. Christians who choose for spiritual reasons to live a life of celibacy are symbolic reminders of this limitless life of love enjoyed in the communion of saints.

26. Will I be able somehow to watch over and protect the loved ones who survive me?

Yes. From the teaching of the communion of saints it is clear that beyond death our relationship with our special loved ones whom we leave behind remains an important part of our life in God. At death we move beyond the limitations that this life imposes on our capacity to love. Our birth into eternity removes the confines that restrict both the quality and quantity of our loving. Simply put, when we enter into the mystery of God, who is love, our loving is itself transformed. It transcends itself. The love we have for our family and friends deepens and broadens beyond what we can even imagine in this life. So those who were dear to us while we were on this Earth are the special beneficiaries of this divine transformation in our capacity to love.

27. Will we learn new things after death?

From the New Testament, it does seem that knowledge will be a dimension of our life in Christ. "For now we see in a mirror, dimly, but then we will see face to face. Now I know only in part; then I will know fully, even as I have been fully known" (1 Cor 13:12). Note how Saint Paul puts self-knowledge at the center of the afterlife. We humans know in a very particular kind of way. We are not just repositories of knowledge like so many data banks. Nor do we know like the animals, whose knowledge resides in the immediacy of the moment. Our knowing is characterized by our abiding experience of knowing that we know. Our knowledge is a dimension of our sense of self. Our knowledge is framed and formed by the contexts of time and history and expectation.

Human knowledge, founded in a sense of self, is essential to human loving. We cannot love what we do not first know. Knowledge is a prerequisite for love. If at death we enter into the mystery of God, who is love, then our capacity for knowledge must continue after death (questions 80, 94, 96, 99, 100).

Since the very nature of human knowing is dynamic and changing, then we can say that we will continue to learn. Our learning in this life, however, is contingent upon time, biology, sensory experience, memory, association, language, and social interaction. How we may continue learning, continue exercising our capacity to know in the next life is not at all certain. But in the passage just quoted from First Corinthians, Saint Paul gives us a hint about the nature of knowledge in the afterlife: it will be bound up with our radically different sense of self; and it will be transformed by God's own way of knowing and loving.

28. Will all my questions be answered?

Well, in light of the answer to question 27, we would have to say yes. But consider this. Questioning is a way of gaining knowledge, a noble philosophical path honored throughout the ages. In fact, if you read the philosophers closely, you often find them trying to get their students to ask better questions, or to ask their questions in better ways. Socrates was always doing this. As we grow older and advance in the spiritual life, something similar happens. Our questions, or the ways we ask them, mature and are deepened by grace, that is, by the action of God's spirit in our minds and hearts. We slowly learn what the really important questions are. We learn to pose them in ways that do not prejudice the answers as much as they used to. Our questioning itself shapes our knowing in more creative, life-giving ways.

So yes, in eternal life our questions will be answered. However, it may be that before we receive those answers, both the questions we ask and how we ask them will have been purified and transformed in ways that we cannot yet imagine. Our bursting into eternity may have undreamt of effects on our inquiring minds to prepare us for knowing "as we are fully known."

Two

Judgment

Judgment in the Bible

29. Is judgment mentioned in the Hebrew scriptures?

Yes. Very often. The ancient Hebrews believed that how they lived was reviewed and judged by God. They were given the Law or Torah, which contained very specific guidelines about how to live in ways that pleased God and that safeguarded the special covenant relationship they enjoyed as God's chosen people. The Law in a sense was their judgment: to keep it was to stay in covenant with God; to break it was to lose that relationship.

So the image of God as judge appears frequently (for example Ps 7:8ff; 119). When the kingdom was established under David and Solomon, judgment became part of the king's responsibility that he shared with God. The kings were supposed to keep the people faithful to the Torah and also to protect the most vulnerable members of their society, namely the poor, widows, children, and resident foreigners. More often than not, the kings of Israel failed in this charge. So God raised up the prophets to call the kings and the people to judgment. As always, the criteria were observance of the Law and just treatment of the weakest in the society (Isa 1–3; Jer 2).

Two developments in later Judaism modified the understanding of God's judgment. One change was the poignant question that runs throughout the Book of Job. If God is just, then why do people who act justly and keep God's Law suffer in this life, while the unjust prosper? Remember that just recompense for one's deeds was understood to happen here and now, on this Earth. Belief in the afterlife was only slowly developing (questions 10, 11, 12). The Book of Job was a challenge to the traditional Jewish confidence in God's justice as fair and reliable.

The second change in Jewish consciousness was the apoca-lyptic movement. Apocalyptic writings raised the possibility of an afterlife and of a just recompense for one's deeds or misdeeds after death. In apocalyptic literature, judgment becomes an important act in the drama of the "last days" or "end time" or "day of the Lord" as it is variously called. A sequence of final events began to emerge in these writings: resurrection of the dead; the end of time and history as we know them; a judgment of all humanity; and, the separation of the just from the unjust for all eternity (Dan 7).

So over the course of time the theme of judgment in Hebrew scriptures develops from daily fidelity to the Law and the prophets into the apocalyptic final judgment on the "day of the Lord" at the end of time. Note that in the Hebrew scriptures there is no clear evidence of a particular judgment immediately after death for indi-viduals. Everything is focused on *the* judgment at the end of time. We do find, however, some descriptions of divine judgment that are not cast in typical apocalyptic language and can be understood to refer to judgment immediately upon death (Wis 3–5).

30. How is judgment understood in the New Testament?

The New Testament is full of references to the apocalyptic idea of a final judgment. It permeates the preaching of Jesus (Matt 11:22–24; 12:41; 16:27; 19:28–29; Mark 13:14–27; Luke 9:26; 10:14; 11:32; 17:22–24,30–37; 21:25–28). Perhaps the most famous text is Jesus' story about the last judgment in Matthew 25, where he describes the separation of the sheep from the goats at the end of time. Jesus takes the criteria of judgment right out of the Law and the prophets: we will be judged on how we treated the least of our brothers and sisters during life.

In John's Gospel there is a unique twist to the theme of judg-ment. John emphasizes that judgment has already occurred (John 5:24; 3:36; 3:18). Our response to the message of Jesus is our judgment. If we accept Jesus' message and believe in him, we are already saved; if we reject him, we are already lost (John 3:19). Situating judgment in the here and now reflects an overall tendency in John's writings to stress the divine immanence, that is, God's pervasive, loving presence in the world. John softens this idea of immediate judgment with a reminder that Jesus came not to judge, but to save (John 3:17; 12:47). So God is present and active in our lives, constantly calling us to share in the divine life. We are continually "judging" ourselves by how we respond or fail to respond to these ever-present divine invitations.

Finally, a major theme in Saint Paul's letters is that we are no longer judged by God on how we may or may not keep the Law or Torah. We are judged—like Abraham, who lived centuries before the Law was ever given to Moses—on our faith in God (Rom 3:21–4:25). Specifically, we are judged on our faith response to the person and message of Jesus who is God among us (Rom 5 and Gal 3:25–29).

Particular Judgment

31. Does the New Testament mention that we are judged by God as soon as we die?

The New Testament hints at the possibility of a preliminary or particular judgment immediately after a person's death. It is suggested in Jesus' parable about the rich man and Lazarus (Luke 16:19–31). The rich man is judged upon his death and found guilty of ignoring the impoverished Lazarus during life. There is no reference to the final, apocalyptic judgment in this parable.

There are also references to judgment in other New Testament books that are not specifically in the apocalyptic mode of the final judgment (Rom 14:10–12; 2 Cor 5:10; Heb 9:27–28). There is, however, no clear teaching in the New Testament about a particular judgment after our death.

32. If the particular judgment of individuals is not a clear teaching in the New Testament, then where did it come from?

As the Christians of the first few centuries began to realize that Jesus might not return any time soon, more and more questions arose about what happens to the deceased in the time after their death and before the final judgment. You can see the hints of such questions even in the very early letter of Paul to the Thessalonians (1 Thess 4:13–18, around 51 CE). Paul assured the Thessalonians that those who had died would not be disadvantaged upon the return of the Lord, but would rise from the dead and join the living to greet Christ.

Over the centuries there have been many theological opinions about what happens to us after death before the end of the world. Some theologians suggested that the soul "sleeps" during this time. In 1336, after centuries of reflection by many theologians, Pope Benedict XII wrote a summary of what he considered the best thinking on this question. It was called *Benedictus Deus* and taught what Catholics still learn today: that after death we are each judged and then immediately enter into heaven, hell, or purgatory. We do not have to wait for the end of time and the final judgment to be with God. This reflects Saint Paul's sentiment when he writes, "My desire is to depart and be with Christ, for that is far better…" (Phil 1:23).

The Eastern Orthodox churches do not hold such a clear and unambiguous teaching about the immediacy of the particular judgment. They prefer to avoid any explicit doctrinal statements about it and about the state of the soul after death before the final judgment at the end of time.

33. Will my judgment after death be like a trial?

The image of a trial is in many religions a long-standing one regarding judgment by God. Even Jesus pictures the Son of man as a judge presiding at a trial when he describes the last judgment

(Matt 25). We have to remember, however, that this image of trial is more an analogy than a literal description.

In fact, this image of trial does not really capture the fullness of what both the Hebrew scriptures and the Christian New Testament mean by God's judgment. Trial involves the presentation and review of evidence, followed by a finding of guilt or innocence. In a biblical sense, judgment is more of an interior discovery than an exterior courtroom proceeding. In Jesus' description of the judgment in Matthew 25, both good and evil persons are surprised by their judgments. They did not realize the implications of their behaviors in this life. It is not as if they had failed in life to distinguish right from wrong. It is rather that during their judgment the full implication and meaning of their deeds becomes evident to them from the divine perspective.

Judgment is an experience of revelation and recognition, an interior illumination by which the deepest significance and consequence of our choices are thrown into stark relief. Many convicted prisoners report something similar to this understanding of judgment. They tell how during months or years of incarceration the deeper truth and meaning of what they did slowly dawn on them and challenge them to take responsibility for it. Their trial is long over. The process of judgment endures for a long time.

Saint John emphasizes that judgment is a continuous process that begins when we first encounter Jesus and his Gospel. It is constantly aided by the Holy Spirit within us (1 John 4:13–16). At the moment of our death when we enter into the unmediated presence of God, divine love drenches our lives with the fullness of eternal light that illumines all we have done or failed to do. We are confronted with the fullness of our self, our personal history, our response to God's presence and power in our lives. All the defenses and denials, the confusion and ignorance that have stood between us and total honesty are burned away by the light of God. We are faced with who we are, or who we have become by our own choices.

34. What will I be judged on?

On the free choices we have made. God is not like a prose-cuting attorney who tries to catch us on technicalities. God respects our free will, yet knows that human choice is almost always a complicated affair with many strands of intertwining intentions, levels of affect, and layers of awareness. We ourselves are often confused about our motivations. As the author of the Book of Wisdom says, we are "weak and short-lived, with little understanding of judgment and laws" (Wis 9:5). God knows us better than we know ourselves. "Even before a word is on my tongue, O Lord, you know it completely" (Ps 139:1–18).

So divine judgment is not a black and white affair that takes account only of external behaviors. God looks into the human heart and sees all its ambiguity. Or we might say that divine judg-ment is an invitation for us to look into our own hearts, to forgive ourselves the weaknesses that lead us into sin and, by the power of grace, to see clearly our intentions—to know them as fully as God does.

35. There are lots of jokes about Saint Peter meeting us at the pearly gates. Will he be involved in my judgment?

Such images are charming, but are totally imaginative mus-ings. There is, however, a good theological reason to think of Saint Peter as somehow involved in our judgment. In Matthew 16:18–19 Jesus says, "You are Peter, and on this rock I will build my church.…I will give you the keys of the kingdom of heaven." Peter, as head of the church, symbolizes the prerogative that the church has regarding judgment of human behaviors, especially the behaviors of its members.

The church exercises a role in judgment not in the sense that pope or priests can come between us and God by usurping the divine role, nor by substituting their judgments for our responsi-bility to examine our internal intentions and motivations. However, the church does have a role to play in how we examine our intentions and how we think about morality. This is called "the formation of conscience." The community of believers, with the advantage of centuries of reflection by theologians and common folk alike, has a great wisdom to offer us as we struggle individually and communally to understand ourselves and our motives, and to choose the right thing to do in any particular situation. The church does "judge" behavior in that sense. It is a partner in our discernment about the rightness or the wrongness of what we do or fail to do.

Saint Peter stands metaphorically at heaven's gate as a reminder that morality in the Christian tradition is not solely a private affair between us and God. It is rather a community struggle and search to discern how best to respond to God's loving covenant with us and the world.

36. Will a last-minute act of contrition really be an advantage at my judgment?

An act of contrition is an admission of one's sinfulness and a prayer for forgiveness. God certainly respects and responds to such an initiative, even if prayed out of fear. So unless it is an act of total hypocrisy—and only God would know that—a last-minute act of contrition may be filled with hope and promise.

Remember, however, what we said about judgment in question 33. An act of contrition does not do away with the kind of self-confrontation and introspection that judgment by its very nature involves. In other words, an act of contrition does not dismiss the review of one's past sins and misdeeds involved in particular judgment and the appreciation of their significance and the extent of their consequences.

Purgatory

37. What is purgatory?

Purgatory is the Catholic Church's teaching that a basically good person who dies might not go immediately to heaven and enter into communion with God. There are two reasons for such a delay: less serious (venial) sins that have not been forgiven or even admitted to by the person; or, more serious (mortal) sins that have been admitted to and forgiven, but whose consequences have not yet been atoned for by repentance of some type. Forgiveness may have been experienced through the sacrament of reconciliation or other sacramental or personal appeals to God.

Purgatory, then, is a state of cleansing from sin and its consequences for a time before one enjoys the "beatific vision" and thereby enters into full union with God (question 100).

38. Is purgatory a place?

No. It can't be, if we understand the soul to be immaterial. Purgatory is better thought of as a state of being. We have already spoken about the difficulties of applying the categories of time and place to the afterlife (question 21). Purgatory is not really a "place" to which souls "go" for more or less "time," like a post-mortem penal colony—though many people imagine it that way and many medieval frescoes portray it as such.

Purgatory is rather a way that Catholic theology tries to reckon with the fact that most of us do not die as saints or martyrs. We take our imperfections and failings with us. If human choices count for something, then we must bear consequences fitted to the varying degrees of sinfulness and sanctity with which we close our lives.

You often hear people talk about difficult times and circumstances in their lives as their "purgatory here on Earth." There is some wisdom in that. Our suffering in this life does cleanse and purify us in many ways: our empathy for others deepens; our motives clarify; our regrets lead us to rectify; our patience grows;

our altruism broadens; our prejudices melt away. If we leave this life with some of this business of spiritual development unattended to, purgatory is a theological way of saying that the process somehow continues after death.

39. So purgatory involves suffering?

That has been the traditional teaching. What suffering might be like after soul leaves body we really don't know. It has been portrayed as fire—a substance that causes pain but also purifies. Fire, however, is only another one of those images we use to reflect on what lies beyond.

It may be helpful to think about the process of judgment itself as at least part of the purgation a soul undergoes after death. We all know how difficult, indeed exquisitely painful and shameful, it can be to admit to ourselves or to others a shortcoming, an addiction, an out-and-out evil deed that we have done. The very process of self-exploration and interior illumination that is involved in the particular judgment may itself be a painful cleansing of the soul, more difficult for those with more to confront, and less so for those who have by grace sought to grow in self-knowledge in this life.

Some theologians over the ages have identified the pain of purgatory to be located in the soul's burning desire to see God. Sin, or the consequences of sin, keeps a soul from union with God for a time, suffering the pain of separation, as if from a lover. This is another way to think about purgatory.

40. Is purgatory mentioned in scripture?

Not explicitly. There is the famous passage in the Second Book of Maccabees: "Therefore he made atonement for the dead, so that they might be delivered from their sins" (2 Macc 12:45). This passage can be used to argue for the idea of purgatory, but in its original context it refers more to the fact that many of the Jewish soldiers who had died defending their homeland against the Syrian Greeks were found to have been carrying small images of a pagan goddess on their persons when they were killed. There is no other reference to purgatory in the Hebrew scriptures.

The word does not appear in the New Testament either. However, certain passages indirectly suggest a forgiveness of sins granted after death (Matt 12:32; 2 Tim 1:18). The efficacy and importance of prayers for the dead emerge in early Christian theological writings as questions about the state of the deceased before the final coming of Christ grew more intense. Saint Augustine in the fifth century presumes that Christians offer such prayers for those who have died (see his Sermon 172.2.2). Purgatory is defined as an explicit Catholic doctrine at the medieval councils of the church at Lyons (1245, and again in 1274) and at Florence (1438). The Council of Trent (1545–1563) defends the teaching of purgatory against the Protestant Reformers who generally dismissed it because the scriptural evidence was so weak.

41. Can we help the souls in purgatory by our prayers?

There is a long tradition of remembering the deceased in our prayers and asking God to forgive their sins and welcome them into divine glory. The text from Second Maccabees mentioned in question 40 is often quoted in this regard. As the idea of purgatory gained more theological ground in the Roman Catholic Church, it became commonplace to associate such prayers with a "reduced stay" in purgatory for those who benefited from such prayers. While it is certainly a good and loving thing to remember those who have gone before us in the faith, we must be careful not to apply time as we know it when thinking of purgatory.

42. What are indulgences?

Indulgences are substitutions or commutations. The church exercised its pastoral prerogative and declared that certain prayers would be the equivalent of so many days, months, or years of fasting and penance. So instead of a penitent having to fast for forty days as penance for a particular sin, the priest confessor could substitute or commute that penance to a few hours of prayer or to the repetition of certain prayers. A certain prayer, for example, would be "worth" or would be the equivalent of forty days of fasting.

The church came up with this system for good pastoral reasons. In fervent efforts to reform the church and society and to stamp out egregious sins, penitential books of the early Middle Ages had developed an intricate system of rather harsh penances that became impossible for penitents to carry through. So the church would grant an indulgence and reduce the penance to make it manageable. These indulgences came to be applied to prayers for the deceased and were soon understood to "deduct" from a soul's "time" in purgatory. Such an approach, however, was really a misdirection of the original nature of indulgences and raises many theological questions.

In 1476, when Pope Sixtus IV needed money for the building of the new St. Peter's Basilica in Rome, he granted the first plenary indulgences applicable to the souls in purgatory for their "immediate release" in exchange for a donation for the new St. Peter's. The recitation of a certain prayer and the gift of a specified amount would "guarantee" a soul in purgatory entrance into heaven. Though he subsequently tried to modify and clarify this practice, the abuse of "selling indulgences" spread quickly and helped to precipitate the Protestant Reformation.

Rome has since stated in 1840 that prayers for the dead, even those identified as "plenary indulgences" depend on God's mercy rather than on human effort, and that we "cannot penetrate this mystery."

43. Do all Christian churches teach about purgatory?

No. It does not appear as a defined doctrine of faith in the Orthodox tradition. Neither do most Protestant denominations today teach it as a necessary article of faith. Martin Luther explicitly taught against it, holding that we are saved solely by Christ's sacrifice and are in need of no further suffering or expiation in order to enter into union with God.

44. Will some people go straight to heaven without having to suffer a time of purgation?

Martyrs for the faith have always been understood to enter immediately into heaven because of their willingness to die for Christ. Also, persons of exemplary faith and morals who die with the benefit of the sacraments have been thought to enter into God's glory immediately upon death.

45. What happens to someone who commits suicide?

Those who take their own lives out of despair or depression seek death as an end to their suffering. We cannot judge them and certainly a loving God knows the depth of their pain. So while the church maintains the objective moral wrong of taking one's own life, subjectively we need to remember that God's justice is always tempered with mercy and that those who have suffered so much are special objects of the divine affection. We might even say that their purgatory may have been on this Earth.

46. What happens to someone who dies in despair, without any hope of an afterlife, even though they were a very good living person?

Again, we cannot know what God intends in such cases. Perhaps purgation for such persons involves the surprising revelation and belated recognition of their own goodness and of what a loving God has prepared for us.

47. What happens to those who die without the benefit of Catholic funeral and burial?

As we mentioned in the answer to question 17, the celebration of the mass of resurrection and other services and prayers for the deceased are celebrations of faith in the risen Christ that benefit mostly the bereaved. Certainly God hears our prayers on behalf of those who have died, and it is to their benefit. However, God's love and mercy are not limited to or by our earthly rituals or petitions. Those who die without benefit of a Christian burial are not by that omission disadvantaged in any way in the divine favor.

Limbo

48. What is limbo?

It's a theological idea that emerged for the first time during a fifth-century theological controversy between Saint Augustine and the British monk Pelagius. In those days it was presumed that unbaptized infants would be denied entrance into heavenly glory because they had not received grace through baptism. Yet neither could they be sent to hell, argued Pelagius, since they had committed no personal sins. So he created the category of *limbo* (a Latin word that means "edge," "hem," or "margin") to describe the state of unbaptized innocents who were never to enjoy communion with God but would dwell in a state of natural happiness. This concept of limbo does not appear anywhere in scripture nor in the previous centuries of Christian writings.

Limbo continued to be discussed and debated by theologians down through the centuries. Questions arose as to whether these deceased little ones suffered in limbo, like the souls in purgatory, or whether they were truly happy and, if so, what was the nature of their happiness. Interestingly, the church has never taught limbo as a doctrine of the faith, and many theologians look upon it as a theological miscarriage.

Unfortunately, in many pastoral and catechetical situations, limbo was taught as if it were an official doctrine of the church, leading to much unnecessary suffering for bereaved parents and families. In many countries unbaptized children were not even allowed to be buried in the consecrated ground of Catholic cemeteries.

There is a second understanding of limbo, found in the writings of the Fathers of the Church, as the place where the just and holy ones from the time before Christ awaited his redemption. It seems related to the Hebrew notion of *sheol* (questions 2 and 64). After the resurrection, in this theological scheme, Christ visited these souls in limbo and took them with him into heavenly glory.

49. Does the Catholic Church still believe in limbo?

As mentioned in the answer to question 48, it never did fully believe in or officially teach limbo as a doctrine of the faith. The word is not even mentioned in the *Catechism of the Catholic Church,* published in 1994. The *Catechism* notes that we should leave the fate of unbaptized infants to the providence and love of God, trusting that God's grace is not limited to baptism, however important that sacrament may be (see par. 1261 in the *Catechism*). Furthermore, a church that champions the life of every fetus as a human being precious to God would seem somehow inconsistent in thinking them consigned to limbo, if not baptized, and thereby eternally deprived of union with God.

It is also notable that among the various funeral rites in the Roman Ritual, there are specific prayers and scriptural readings designated to be used at the funeral mass "for a child who died before baptism." One of them prays that the parents be comforted with the knowledge that the child for whom they grieve "is entrusted now to your loving care."

Some theologians may want to continue to debate the idea of limbo in reflecting on the fate of unbaptized children, but the general sense of the faithful is that it was a bad idea from the start.

50. What happens to fetuses or infants who die so young? Do they remain at that stage of development?

Perhaps the best response to this question is from Saint John: "Beloved, we are God's children now; what we will be has not yet been revealed. What we do know is this: when he is revealed, we will be like him for we will see him as he is" (1 John 3:2). Christian faith and Catholic teaching urge us to respect the human life that is wrapped in the tenderness of the womb or held in the vulnerability of infancy and young childhood. Human life at all stages is precious to God. Over the centuries theologians have suggested that those who die before birth, or during infancy, or before the age of reason reach their potential for human knowing and loving after death, and so are brought by God into the fullness of heavenly joy (question 93). Judgment for them is a special kind of revelation and recognition (question 33) that prepares them to be like God and to see and know God fully, even as they are known by God.

51. What happens to those who are not Christians?

The church teaches that baptism is the Christian's ordinary and necessary way into the mystery of the risen Christ. However, those who have never heard of Christ nor come to understand the message of the gospel are certainly not beyond God's love and grace. Such persons who seek truth and who live according to God's will as they understand it are judged on how they have lived. Catholic theology has spoken of the "baptism of desire," which is a theological way of saying that if such persons knew the importance of baptism, they would request it. Catechumens, candidates preparing for baptism, are also saved by their desire for the sacrament if they should die before receiving it (see the *Catechism of the Catholic Church,* pars. 1259 and 1260).

The End of the World and the Last Judgment

52. Can we know when the end of the world will be?

"But about that day and hour no one knows, neither the angels of heaven, nor the Son, but only the Father," was Jesus' answer to this question (Matt 24:36; Mark 13:32; also, 1 Thess 5:1–2). Over the centuries people have ignored Jesus' admonition about predicting the end of the world and the final judgment, and have tried to piece together evidence from the Bible to do just that. Such activity reaches a fevered pitch around the turn of a century or millennium, or when world events make our situation seem especially precarious. The Bible itself is generally more interested in predicating meaning to history than in predicting the end of it.

53. Doesn't Jesus himself speak about the end of time and his second coming?

He does. Especially in Matthew 24, Mark 13, and Luke 21. These chapters present remnants of Jesus' preaching that are full of apocalyptic themes. In Mark 13, Jesus says that the destruction of the Temple in Jerusalem will immediately precede his return or *parousia,* a Greek word that means "presence" or "coming."

In Matthew 24, the emphasis is also on the destruction of the Temple, but more as a theological reminder of the impermanence of this world and the eventual return of Christ at the end of time. Remember that the Romans did destroy the Temple in 70 CE. The very early Christians, many of whom were themselves Jewish, were traumatized by that cataclysmic event in Jewish history. They looked back and searched through accounts of Jesus' preaching to try to comprehend what had happened.

In Luke 21, Jesus speaks of the destruction not only of the Temple but of the entire city of Jerusalem because of its rejection of Jesus. Luke's point is that after the destruction of Jerusalem, Christians will travel around the world to preach the gospel and prepare all humanity for Jesus' return.

54. Did the early Christians expect Jesus to return soon?

Yes. In Mark's Gospel, which was written probably between 65 and 70 CE, we have evidence that the earliest Christians fully expected Jesus to return during their lifetime, in fact, shortly after the destruction of the Temple. This expectation of Jesus' imminent return is also found in 1 Thessalonians 4:13–18, where Saint Paul in his very first letter (around 51 CE) consoles believers who have lost loved ones. He assures them that their beloved departed will not be disadvantaged by death, but will be raised from the dead to join their living relatives in greeting Jesus upon his return.

This impatient expectation of Jesus' return is also found at the climax of the Book of Revelation in the repeated promise of Jesus, "I am coming soon" (Rev 22:7,20), and in the joyful response of believers, "Amen. Come, Lord Jesus" (Rev 22:20).

As time moved on, however, the next generation or two of early Christians began to realize that the second coming of Christ, or the *parousia,* was not going to happen any time soon. This growing realization is reflected in Matthew 24 and Luke 21, which we discussed in question 53. In those chapters, Jesus' return is no longer expected immediately after the destruction of the Temple or of the city of Jerusalem. Rather, those catastrophic events serve as theological reminders of the second coming.

In chapter 3 of the Second Letter of Peter, we have an explicit theological reflection on this delay in Jesus' return that so concerned the second and third generations of Christians. The author reminds his readers "that with the Lord one day is like a thousand years, and a thousand years are like one day. The Lord is not slow about his promise, as some think of slowness, but is patient with you, not wanting any to perish, but all to come to repentance" (2 Pet 3:8–9). This passage emphasizes the idea that time is a human category that does not apply to God as it does to us, and that we should concentrate on conforming our lives to God's love and grace.

Christians still wait for Jesus' second coming at the end of time, even though our anticipation is not of an immediate event as it was for those first generations of believers. Our belief in his return, celebrated especially during the Advent season, helps to keep us open to and expectant of God's continuing presence and power in our world.

55. Does the Book of Revelation give us a description of the end of the world?

Not exactly. The Book of Revelation, or the Apocalypse as it is also called, does indeed have many vivid descriptions of worldwide distress and upheaval in the heavens (Rev 6; 8; and 9). We can understand many of these passages much better when we consider why and for whom Revelation was written.

During the first century, Christians suffered intense persecution under the emperors Nero (54–68 CE) and Domitian (81–96 CE). Many of the cosmic actions and striking symbols in Revelation are covert references to this painful situation. As persecuted groups often do, the early Christians spoke and wrote about their suffering and their hopes for release in secret code and symbolic language. The secrecy was to prevent even more persecution and reprisals. So the accounts of the heavens collapsing and Earth being destroyed are a suffering people's wrenching cries for the social order to be overturned so that their persecutors might fall from their positions of power and domination.

Revelation uses many of the same symbols found in the in the Hebrew Book of Daniel. Daniel was written in the fourth century BCE to encourage and comfort the Jews during their persecution by Epiphanes, the Syrian Greek king who brutally slaughtered thousands of Jewish people. Much of the language about "the end of the present age" and a "new world to come" has to be understood in light of the historical contexts that produced the apocalyptic writings of Daniel and Revelation. These parts of sacred scripture—both Hebrew (Daniel) and Christian (Revelation)—express the longing of the persecuted to see revolutionary changes, initiated by God, that would end their sufferings and restore justice.

56. So does Revelation have anything to do with the end of the world and the last judgment?

The original historical context of the Book of Revelation (explained in question 55) does not mean that this part of scripture has nothing to do with the end of time and the second coming of Christ. The occasion of violence and ravage suffered by local communities of Christians under Rome became the occasion for poetic and symbolic reflections about the end and purpose of history itself. No matter what our particular situation or circumstance in this world, Revelation reminds us that we are moving toward a new creation. "Then I saw a new heaven and a new earth..." (Rev 21:1).

Revelation emerged amid the cries of a persecuted Christian community. Yet it is also a constant reminder to all Christians that "we have here no lasting city" (Heb 13:14), and that Christ will return to "make all things new" (Rev 21:5). In a sense, Revelation, the last book of the New Testament, tells how the story of creation, begun in the first book of the Bible, Genesis, will be completed. Christ, the Word of God, who was present at creation and through whom all things were made, will bring all things to their ultimate end in God. "I am the Alpha and the Omega, the first and the last," says the risen Christ (Rev 1:8; 21:6; 22:12).

Undue fixation on Revelation's bizarre symbols and repetitive sets of numbers (lots of fours, sevens, twelves, and twenty-fours) may occasionally sell sensational books and spawn B movies. Scrupulous study of the text for secret codes and hidden messages to interpret current events may incite millennial movements. Such things, however, only distract us from Revelation's real challenge: to remain open to the saving power of God in history, even in the midst of evil times and great suffering; and to live Christian lives that help make this world more just and peaceful, while we journey toward the fulfillment of creation as God intends. So in that sense Revelation does have a lot to do with the end and purpose of history.

57. Who or what are the "antichrist" and the "beast"?

The word *antichrist* appears only in the First and Second Letters of John. In those texts it seems to refer to a person or persons who are misrepresenting Christ or teaching against him or against the church (1 John 2:18,22; 4:3; 2 John 7). In Revelation the word *antichrist* is not used. Rather, the enemy of Christ and the church is called "the beast" (Rev 13:1ff and 19:19ff) and "the whore of Babylon" (Rev 17; 18). These two unpleasant figures seem to be a direct reference to the Roman emperor or to the empire itself.

So in their original scriptural contexts, these enemies of Christ and the church are either false teachers who threaten the community of believers from within with their misguided ideas (the antichrist), or external persecutors who terrorize, imprison, and murder the faithful (the beast).

Over the centuries the idea of the antichrist has been used (or misused) to vilify heretics. It has also served to brand particularly ruthless and cruel demagogues of history, such as Hitler or Stalin or Pol Pot. It is not a reference to Satan, nor is it meant to foreshadow an ultimate evildoer who will threaten the world toward its end.

The image of the beast emerges from scripture as a constant reminder that Christians and all people of goodwill must deal with and oppose those whose selfishness and pathology will wreak havoc on the world. This struggle between God's faithful and evildoers will continue until the end when evil is finally overcome (Rev 19:20).

58. What is Armageddon and what does it have to do with the end of the world?

Armageddon (or Harmageddon) is mentioned only once in the Bible (Rev 16:16). It is the site of the final battle between good over evil, and an assurance that in the end good will prevail. Scripture scholars are not certain if the word *Armageddon,* which is Hebrew in origin, refers to a specific place. It could be a reference to the area around Megiddo or possibly in the region of Mount Carmel, both sites of many conflicts between the Hebrews of old and their political or religious enemies.

The geography is less important than the deeper meaning. In highly symbolic language that alludes to the history of epic biblical battles, the author of Revelation proclaims that in the end all that is good will triumph and all that is evil will be destroyed. The word *Armageddon* has come to refer to any epic, deciding battle. It is also used as a shorthand literary reference to the violent end of the world.

59. God seems very angry throughout the Book of Revelation. Why?

At one level, the anger is that of the persecuted communities out of which Revelation emerged as a sacred text. At another level, Revelation is God's answer to the question posed in the Book of Job. Remember that for the author of Job, retribution for one's deeds had to happen during this life, since there was at that time no established belief in an afterlife except *sheol* (question 29). The Book of Revelation is a resounding affirmation that in the end, and beyond this life, wrong will be righted, evildoers will be punished, and the just will be rewarded eternally. God's anger is part of the divine triumph over evil. Perhaps God's anger in Revelation resonates more with readers who themselves are victims of injustice, poverty, and power politics.

Amid the divine anger in Revelation there are surprisingly beautiful images of judgment. The final judgment is symbolically referred to as a harvest that God himself reaps with his sickle (Rev 14). The same passage also offers us the image of a yield of grapes that God presses into new wine. Harvests and vineyards are reminiscent of Jesus' many parables about the kingdom of God. They are also reminders of the bread and wine of the Christian Eucharist that we celebrate in anticipation of Jesus' return and the establishment of the kingdom of God.

60. I know that some Christians talk about a "thousand-year reign of Christ" before his second coming and the end of the world. What is that about?

Revelation says that at an as yet undetermined point in history, Satan will be held bound and powerless for a thousand years, during which time good will prevail, the gospel will be preached, and all evil overcome. At the end of these thousand years, Satan will be released to "deceive the nations" (Rev 20:8). Then Christ will return for the last judgment and the final victory over evil (Rev 20:11–15).

Some theologians in the early centuries of the church interpreted this obscure passage literally. Even today some Christian sects such as the Anabaptists, Adventists, and Jehovah's Witnesses continue to do so. This teaching is called "millenarianism" or "chiliasm," referring to the period of one thousand years. Most Christian churches do not take this passage literally.

61. Some Christians believe in predestination. Does that mean that God already knows who will be saved and who won't?

The teaching of predestination actually does not rest upon the belief that God *already knows* who is saved and who is not saved. Strictly speaking, the classical understanding of predestination is that God *has already willed* who is saved and who is not saved. Predestination is a somewhat awkward theological teaching that emphasizes in the strongest way possible that our salvation depends entirely on God's willing it.

This idea first gets wide theological currency in the writings of Saint Augustine in the fifth century. In his long argument with the Pelagians, who thought that we proved ourselves worthy of salvation by our spiritual striving and efforts, Augustine retorted that we are saved *only* by God's will and grace.

In pressing this argument as far as he could, Augustine passionately declared that God is absolutely free and sovereign in the dispensation of grace. Our salvation is completely in the hands of God, since we can do nothing—nor can we even conceive of what to do—in order to be saved unless God gives us the grace. Augustine goes on: God has *willed* from all eternity a certain fixed number of those who will be saved. Augustine and subsequent Christian writers appeal to Paul's Letter to the Romans where he writes about those whom God has *predestined* to be justified and glorified (Rom 8:28–30). (Certainly other interpretations of this text are possible.)

Many other theologians, especially in the Eastern Orthodox churches, found Augustine's theology of predestination to violate the equally important doctrine of human freedom. They reject the idea that God has chosen only some people to be saved. These theologians point to the First Letter to Timothy, which speaks of a God "who desires everyone to be saved and to come to the knowledge of the truth" (1 Tim 2:4). Nonetheless, the idea of predestination gained theological currency and persisted throughout the ages. It was revived and reiterated by the Protestant Reformers Luther and Calvin, both greatly influenced by Saint Augustine's writings. It can still be found in the popular and academic theology of some Protestant churches in the Calvinist tradition.

Since the Reformation, Catholic theology has tried to balance the idea behind predestination—God's absolute, mysterious, impenetrable, and infinite being, knowing and loving—with the necessity of preserving human freedom by which we each respond to God's will that we be saved. How successful various theologians have been in their attempts is debatable.

Perhaps it is not Augustine's doctrinal writings about predestination that are most helpful here, but his pastoral sermons and letters. In them he counsels his people not to worry about predestination, and not to fret about whether they as individuals have been predestined to be saved or not. Maybe he himself had begun to realize how this convoluted and paradoxical teaching could be used rather uncharitably against one's enemies by presuming them to be among the *massa damnata* (those predestined not to be saved). We should simply pray, says Augustine, for the grace of persevering in our faith, hope, and love.

62. What will a final or last judgment at the end of time add to the particular judgment we undergo at death?

The two judgments will both be about the same *content,* namely, how we have lived our lives on this Earth. The last or general judgment at the end of time will not be like an appeals court wherein God might overturn our particular judgment because of new evidence or a procedural violation.

The two judgments will be different, however, because of *context*. At the general judgment, all human beings will have lived and died and made their choices. With the fullness of human volition and the completion of history, the totality of interrelationship among all created persons and things will be revealed and recognized. The particular judgment reveals to us how our lives have impacted others and the world we have inhabited. The general judgment will reveal the interrelationships among the entire human family over the full course of its history. Our individual lives will be situated in the widest possible context and understood from a perspective of finality—something that would not be a dimension of our particular judgments before the end of time and history.

There is, however, that problem of time once again. If when we die we leave time and space as we know them, then the distinction just made between particular judgment and general judgment might best be held tentatively. The logic of the distinction may help us reflect here and now on such mysteries. How much it actually applies to what God has prepared for us we do not know.

THREE

———————————————

HELL

Hell in the Bible

63. Is hell mentioned in the Hebrew scriptures?

The early Hebrews had the concept of *sheol,* an underground realm of existence after death. It was a land of darkness, gloom, and forgetfulness to which all humans go after death, regardless of how well or ill they live (question 2). It is poetically and poignantly described in the Book of Isaiah by King Hezekiah: "For Sheol cannot thank you, death cannot praise you; those who go down into the Pit cannot hope for your faithfulness" (Isa 38:18).

The Hebrew idea of *sheol* is similar to Hades in Greek mythology and to the notion of *Helle* found among the ancient Germanic tribes. These various early understandings of the afterlife did not discriminate between good and evil, nor did they involve the idea of reward or punishment after death. They are simply imaginative attempts to wrestle with what may await us beyond death.

What most people today would understand by hell, the place of the demons and the damned, emerges late in the Hebrew scriptures. The word *gehenna* begins to appear after 500 BCE as a place where evildoers—Jew and Gentile—are punished after death. *Gehenna* was originally the name of Jerusalem's city dump in the Valley of Hinnon. In ancient times it had been the site of human sacrifice (Jer 7:31). In late prophetic literature and in apocalyptic Jewish writings it is described in great detail as a place of darkness, everlasting fire, undying worms, chains, and all sorts of gory punishments (Isa 24; 2 Esdras 7:36; Enoch 27:2; 90:24–26). Eventually *gehenna* is understood as a part of *sheol* where evil people, even before the final resurrection of the dead, suffer a wide range of punishments fitted to their deeds in life (Isa 66:24; 2 Macc 6:26ff).

The Book of Wisdom also teaches that evildoers will be punished in the afterlife (Wis 4:18–19). There is no systematic teaching about hell in the Hebrew scriptures, just as there is no uniform, dogmatic belief about the afterlife in Judaism even today (see questions 2, 10, 11, 12). Yet by the time of Jesus there was among the Jews widespread acceptance of the idea of punishment in the afterlife for those who deserved it.

64. Is hell mentioned in the Christian New Testament?

The Hebrew word *gehenna,* as a place of fearful punishment of the wicked, appears often in the Synoptic Gospels (Matthew, Mark, and Luke). John the Baptist alludes to it (Matt 3:12). Jesus both mentions and describes *gehenna* many times in his teaching (Matt 5:29ff; 6:22; 8:12; 10:28; 13:42; 13:50; 18:9; 22:12; 23:15; 23:33; 24:51; 25:30; Mark 9:43ff; 11:23; Luke 10:15; 12:5; 13:28). He also uses the word *sheol* (*Hades* in the Greek texts) several times (Matt 11:23; Luke 10:18; 16:23).

Neither *gehenna* nor *sheol* is found in John's Gospel. However, in John's writings Jesus speaks of banishment to the darkness for evildoers (John 3:19–21). Punishment is essentially exclusion from the life of God offered to us through Jesus (John 8:24; 10:28).

In his letters Saint Paul admonishes that evildoers will suffer eternal destruction, anguish, and separation from the presence and glory of God (2 Thess 1:9; Rom 2:9; 9:22; Phil 3:19). The dramatic and disturbing imagery of hell found in Jewish apocalyptic writings reappears in the later books of the New Testament (2 Pet 2:17; Jude 6–7) and especially in Revelation, which describes a lake of fire and sulfur where the devil and evildoers suffer forever (Rev 19:10; 21:8).

So, yes, the idea of hell is taken seriously in the New Testament by Jesus and by his earliest followers. They inherited it largely from Jewish apocalyptic literature.

65. How could Jesus have "descended into hell" before he rose again on the third day as it says in the creed?

Some professions of faith or creeds, such as the Apostles' Creed, proclaim that after his death Jesus "descended into hell." Hell in these texts is a translation of the idea of *sheol,* not *gehenna* (question 63). Thus this creedal statement says two things: that like all human beings Jesus died and shared completely in our human fate (question 5); and, that he brought redemption to all the good souls waiting in *sheol* (question 49).

Catholic Teaching about Hell

66. What does the Catholic Church teach about hell?

From New Testament times, the church has always taught that those who die in grievous or mortal sin are deprived forever of union with God and also suffer eternal punishment. This teaching has been reaffirmed over the centuries by various documents, such as the fifth-century *Fides Damasi,* and by several councils of the church, such as Lateran IV (1215), Lyons II (1274), Florence (1439), and Trent (1547). In 1336 Pope Benedict XII wrote in his papal constitution *Benedictus Deus* that the damned go to hell immediately upon death after their individual, particular judgment, even before the final or general judgment of all humankind (question 32).

The church has also distinguished between two kinds of punishment in hell. *Passive punishment*—the worse of the two—is separation from God, which is the essence of hell. *Positive punishment* involves all of the pain and suffering the person endures throughout their whole being because of this deprivation. This distinction is reaffirmed in the 1979 "Letter on Certain Questions Concerning Eschatology" published by the Vatican's Sacred Congregation for the Doctrine of the Faith.

Beyond these general statements, there is no official church teaching on what hell may be like. Though theologians over the centuries have sometimes concluded from the Bible that hellfire is real and physical, the magisterium or teaching authority of the church has rarely made official declarations on how to interpret this and other apocalyptic imagery of hell (though see question 67 following).

67. Is hell a physical place?

On Wednesday, July 28, 1999, Pope John Paul II surprised a lot of people gathered for his weekly audience with a message about hell. (Perhaps the summer heat in Italy prompted his remarks!) He stated that we must not interpret apocalyptic imagery about hell literally, but symbolically. He went on to say that hell is not a physical place, but a state. It is the freely chosen "self-exclusion from communion with God and the blessed" (see also the *Catechism of the Catholic Church,* par. 1033).

Damnation is not, the pope claimed, a result of God's initiative, but of a human being's free-will choice to reject God's love. In this sense hell and its suffering begin already in this life. This unexpected papal commentary on the Catholic theology of hell helps clarify centuries of church teaching and theological speculation. It also upsets many Christians, Catholics and others, who prefer a literal understanding of hell as a physical place of real fire and physical torture. Though he was not speaking infallibly and proclaiming official church dogma, the pope was weighing in on long-standing theological speculations about hell and suggesting a direction for future reflections on the topic.

68. What about all those ancient and medieval paintings or descriptions of hell?

They draw heavily from the apocalyptic imagery of hell in the Hebrew and Christian scriptures. Artists have also relished exquisite, detailed tortures tailored to each of the seven capital sins (pride, lust, anger, covetousness, envy, sloth, and gluttony).

A high point—or low point, depending on your perspective—of hellish imagery is found in Dante's great fourteenth-century poetic masterpiece *The Divine Comedy.* In Book I, *Inferno,* he describes nine circles or layers inhabited by the damned. The deeper one descends, the more wicked are those condemned to that level and the more intense their punishments. Dante pulls a symbolic switch by assigning encompassing ice—not fire—to the deepest level of hell and its most evil inhabitants.

Michelangelo's *Last Judgment* on the front wall of the Sistine Chapel is another masterpiece inspired by traditional apocalyptic themes and classical literature. The powerful imagery of Michelangelo's art and Dante's poetry has helped to shape the popular image of hell even to this day.

69. After the resurrection of the dead and the final judgment, will hell be different?

This question presumes to apply our human category of time to the afterlife. We must proceed then with any response tentatively, knowing that the distinctions we might make are provisional at best. We could reflect, however, on the themes of completion and corporality.

At the resurrection of the dead, with the end of time and history and the judgment of humanity, all creation will be renewed and completed in Christ (Col 1:15–20; Eph 1:8–10; see also question 62). Human free will, an essential and dramatic dimension of history, will have been resolved as part of the disposition of all things and the fulfillment of creation. Human choice, as a variable and unpredictable factor of history, will cease with the end of time. So in this sense no one will be "added to" the population of hell after the final judgment.

With the resurrection of the body, physicality will somehow complete our experience of "a new heaven and a new earth" (Rev 21:1) and intensify our enjoyment of divine love. For the condemned, conversely, the retrieval of physicality will heighten their experience of separation from God and exclusion from the fulfillment of creation.

So, questions of time kept apart, the themes of completion and corporality point to some qualitative difference in the afterlife upon the final judgment.

70. Are Catholics required to believe in hell?

If by *hell* you mean a physical place of endless fire and tortuous punishments, no. If by *hell* you mean a final state of being and human experience apart from God that results from total selfishness and the free-choice rejection of love and goodness, then yes.

Hell is a theological consequence of three things: belief in the afterlife, affirmation of free will, and the attribution of retributive justice. If we believe that our choices do matter, that over time our behavior defines who we are, reveals what we value, and distinguishes our capacity for love, then we must somehow allow for the terrible reality of those whose lifestyles slowly diminish their being, devalue their person, and extinguish their love. Hell is the final end and consequence of such a life. Catholic teaching affirms the possibility of such a state.

The Devil and the Fallen Angels

71. Are devils mentioned in Hebrew scriptures?

Like most ancient peoples, the Hebrews presumed a realm of undefined supernatural "heavenly beings" (see Job 1:6). These beings were not always helpful or friendly to human beings, but they remained under God's sovereignty. There are a variety of such demons or devils throughout Hebrew scriptures.

Some of these beings are described as wild supernatural creatures that haunt the desert wasteland and threaten human beings who are unfortunate enough to encounter them (Isa 13:21; 34:14; Tob 8:3; Zech 5:8–11). Often the idols of other tribes or nations are called demons (Deut 32:17; Ps 106:37). Most often, demons are powerful creatures who tempt, disturb, accuse, or otherwise harass God's people (1 Sam 16:14; Zech 3:1; Job 1). The name *Satan* comes from a Hebrew word that means "accuser" (as in Job 1:6ff). *Diabolos,* which also means "accuser" or "opponent," was the Greek translation for the Hebrew word *Satan* and is the origin of the English word *devil.*

Jewish apocalyptic literature introduces the idea of a cosmic battle between God and all the forces of evil in the cosmos. Out of that context the figure of one dominating evil spirit that lords it over all the others begins to emerge. This Satan becomes the prince of those angels who also opposed God and were expelled from heaven along with their leader. Satan becomes the prototype or model for hell's population of all those who reject God's will and love.

72. Doesn't Satan figure prominently in the New Testament?

Yes, and you can see the influence of both earlier Hebrew scriptures and later Jewish apocalyptic writings on how the New Testament authors present Satan and demons. Jesus first encounters Satan in the desert wilderness, as his Jewish ancestors might have (Matt 4:1ff; Mark 1:12–13; Luke 4:1ff). There the devil tempts him but Jesus resists, signaling the coming victory over evil in the kingdom of God (Luke 22:31; John 13:2,27).

The demonic possession of persons is not found in Hebrew scriptures. It is common, however, in nonbiblical Jewish apocalyptic literature and from there enters the New Testament. When Jesus casts out demons, it is a further sign of the impending victory of God over all evil, suffering, and sin (Matt 8:16; Mark 1:34; Luke 6:18; 11:14). Jesus' passion and death are the devil's final defeat (Luke 22:3,31; John 12:31; 13:27; 1 Cor 2:8).

Saint John does not report Jesus casting out demons, but he frequently uses darkness as a symbol of evil (John 1:5; 3:19; 8:12; 9:1–41; 12:35–36; 13:30; 1 John 1:11). In John's Gospel, the devil is "the father of lies" (John 8:44), the "ruler of the world" (John 12:31), or simply "the evil one" (John 17:15). In what may be a reference to demons or their influence, Saint Paul writes about cosmic beings that he calls "principalities, authorities and powers" that rival God but that Christ conquers (Rom 8:38; 1 Cor 15:24; 2 Cor 11:14; Eph 1:21; 6:12). Demons are also identified with the false gods of other peoples (1 Cor 10:20–21) and with the "divining spirits" popular among a superstitious populace throughout the Roman Empire (Acts 16:16–18).

73. Doesn't Satan appear in the Book of Revelation?

It is in Revelation that many of these various and sometimes disconnected manifestations of evil are brought together using the categories of Jewish and Christian apocalyptic literature. In Revelation 12 the devil is presented as a dragon (an apocalyptic symbol of evil, also found in Babylonian, Egyptian, and Greek myths). The devil is identified as the lying serpent of Genesis 3:15 that tricked Eve and Adam (Rev 12:9; 20:2; see also Wis 2:24). He is the demonic controller of human society, specifically dominating the Roman Empire symbolized by the beast and the whore (Rev 17).

The archangel Michael, who is the great defender of Israel in Jewish apocalyptic literature (Dan 10:12–21; 12:1) defeats Satan and expels him from heaven (Rev 12:7–8). Revelation also tells of Satan's final defeat and eternal banishment to hell (Rev 20:10).

In general we can say that the New Testament takes the existence of evil and of evil powers very seriously. The various manifestations, embodiments, and personifications of evil powers that we find in Hebrew scriptures are also found in the New Testament. Especially in the Book of Revelation, these creatures assume the form that most Christians would recognize today as the fallen angels we call Satan and his demons.

74. What about Beelzebub?

Beelzebub (Mark 3:22), which means "Lord of the flies," appears in the fourth-century Latin Vulgate translation of the Bible. From there it passed into English as a popular name for the devil. For the ancient Hebrews it had been a derogatory name for Ekron, the god of their longtime neighbors the Philistines (2 Kgs 1:2,3,6,16).

There is also the slightly different (and probably more original) spelling *Beelzebul*, which was used in earlier manuscripts of the New Testament. It is a linguistic corruption of *Baalzabub*, which was the name and title—meaning "Lord of the Earth"—of the chief Canaanite god Baal. The Canaanites were longtime, idol-worshiping neighbors of the Hebrews. To appropriate the name of an idol for an evil spirit was a common practice for the Hebrews (question 71).

75. What does the church teach about the devil?

Given the great extent of its teaching on faith and morals, the church has said relatively little about Satan and demons. Official church teaching about the devil can be summed up in a few main points. The church has accepted scriptural testimony about the existence of evil forces and spirits; warned of the influence such beings can have over our sinful human nature; affirmed that such beings are creatures and not in any way equal or threatening to the Creator; and, testified to Christ's complete victory over all forms of evil. The church has never defined *what* Satan is, other than a fallen angel.

Satan, temptation, and the power of evil are themes that appear regularly in the writings of the Fathers of the Church and of medieval theologians, especially in their commentaries on scripture. They also present the Christian sacraments as effective defenses against the powers of evil. The church has offered exorcism as a ritual (though not a sacrament) for persons judged to be troubled by forces that elude human understanding or medical diagnosis. In general the church emphasizes pastoral care and prayerful encouragement as the preferred ways to help deliver people from evil.

76. Are Catholics required to believe in the devil?

None of the creeds of the church mention Satan as an article of faith. From ancient times, however, the liturgy of baptism has called upon initiates and the assembled Christian community "to reject Satan and all his works" and all the power and allure of evil. So while the church affirms the existence of evil spirits, and of a chief evil one among them, this teaching is not emphasized as primary or even as essential to the Gospel. Evil is less a matter of divine revelation and more a realistic assessment of human experience. Evil spirits are found in many religions and are not exclusive to Christian revelation or doctrine.

In past centuries the devil was in the forefront of the preaching and teaching of many Christian theologians, such as Martin Luther. Many people today find the existence of Satan and other demons difficult to accept as anything more than the mythology of prescientific civilizations past. However, as contemporary science opens our minds to the immensity and variety of the universe, it is at least not illogical to entertain the possibility of cosmic powers of evil that may inhabit it.

The Fate of the Damned

77. What is the unforgivable sin that the Bible talks about?

The idea of an "unforgivable sin" appears in the gospel story about Jesus' confrontation with a hostile crowd that questioned the source of his authority and his power to cast out demons (Mark 3:28–30; Matt 12:31–32). Jesus' response to their challenge was threefold. First, he affirms that God will forgive all sins, even blasphemy (Mark 3:28; Matt 12:31). Second, even those who criticize or blaspheme him will be forgiven (Matthew 12:32). Third, those *who blaspheme or speak against the Holy Spirit can never be forgiven,* "either in this age or in the age to come" (Matt 12:32). They are "guilty of an eternal sin" (Mark 3:29).

Strong and definitive language. Also seemingly contradictory. How can God forgive *all* sins, and yet at the same time *not* forgive this one particular sin of blasphemy against the Holy Spirit? What exactly is blasphemy against the Holy Spirit? Why is it such an exceptional sin and why so different from blaspheming Jesus himself?

To *blaspheme* means to speak irreverently against God or to revile God. Jesus is willing to accept and forgive people's lack of understanding of the gospel or their rejection of himself. In the theological language of the New Testament, however, the Holy Spirit is a way of speaking about God's offering of self, the divine invitation to intimate communion, God's gift of eternal, unconditional love. So, we might mess up our own lives and the lives of others. We may misinterpret or even reject the gospel of Jesus. Yet so long as we remain open at some level of our being to divine love, then God will find a way into our souls to heal and forgive and make us whole.

It is only when we revile the very notion of divine love or resist the possibility of divine initiative that we risk making ourselves impervious even to God, who respects our will. The unforgivable sin is a result of our own refusal of God's advances to us, not of God's withdrawal from us. It is unforgivable because God will not violate our freedom. In a sense, condemnation to hell is the fate of those who at the most profound level of their being freely reject the possibility of divine love.

78. Can we be certain that someone who lived a decidedly evil life, like Hitler, is in hell?

No. The church has never taught that any human being is definitely condemned to hell. So, while we are asked to accept the reality of true evil and the possibility of damnation, we cannot presume that even the vilest of persons has willingly remained closed to God at the moment of death.

On the other hand, the church regularly proclaims and celebrates many people as saints or "citizens of heaven" living in eternal communion with the Holy One.

79. Is hell really going to last forever, eternally?

It can be difficult to accept that God would allow any person to end up eternally separated from the divine reality, in a state of endless deprivation and suffering. The great third-century theologian Origen (185–254 CE) taught that in the end hell itself will be destroyed and all condemned persons and even the fallen angels that we call devils will be restored to relationship with God. The church rejected this theory of final restoration and reintegration of evil persons and fallen angels (called *apocatastasis* in Greek). However, the need for such an official rejection by the Synod of Constantinople in 543 shows how attractive this idea can be.

Perhaps, some claim, those who die condemned by their own choices simply cease to exist after a life of evil deeds. Christian teaching, however, puts such an emphasis on the sanctity and mystery of each person that annihilation of any soul by God has never gained much of a foothold in the history of theology. Yet it might be instructive to imagine hell as a state of being *faced with nothingness* forever.

80. Will people in hell know each other?

There is no church teaching on this question. All we might do is to extrapolate from the church's limited theological understanding of hell as eternal separation from God (questions 64, 66, 67).

In his First Letter Saint John writes, "God is love, and those who abide in love abide in God and God in them" (1 John 4:16). Absolute separation from God means a complete absence of love, either for oneself or others. Knowledge is both a prerequisite for love and a continuing dimension of the act of loving. By love we affirm and value the one we know. Informed loving prompts us to learn more about the beloved. Knowledge and love are thus intimately intertwined and interdependent dimensions of human experience.

Without love knowledge is sterile, frustrated, isolating, and perhaps ultimately destructive of self and others. If we can claim theologically that there is no love in hell, then we can say that whatever knowledge the damned may have of one another, or indeed of God, is devoid of interpersonal acceptance, recognition, or company of any type. The saying "Misery loves company" would not then apply to the damned. For company implies some recognition of and empathy for the other's suffering.

The French existentialist philosopher Jean-Paul Sartre comments on hell in his play *No Exit*. One of the characters cynically remarks, with hesitation, that "hell is—other people." Theologically we might say in response, with hesitation and sadness, that "in hell other people—just don't matter."

Four

Heaven

Heaven in the Bible

81. Is heaven mentioned in the Hebrew scriptures?

Yes, very often; but the meaning is somewhat different from the popular understanding of heaven today. When the ancient Hebrews looked up and saw the sky, they imagined it to be a huge inverted bowl that covered the Earth (which they thought was flat). They called this dome the firmament (*raquia'* in Hebrew). Above this solid firmament God stored the rain and snow that fell to Earth through holes in the firmament (Gen 1:8; Ps 148:4–6). The planets and stars were suspended from this curved, vaulted ceiling (Gen 1:14–18). This was the Hebrews' prescientific cosmology or way of understanding the universe.

The word *heaven* (*shamayim* in Hebrew) was used to refer to the sky, to the lofty firmament or dome *(raquia')* above the sky, and also to the space above the firmament. The Hebrews believed that God dwells "in the heavens" and specifically *above* the firmament (Ps 104:2–3,13). The divine throne rested on the top of the firmament (Isa 66:1; Exod 24:10). From time to time God would "come down" from the heavens to intervene in human affairs and to meet with Moses or the Hebrew people (Gen 11:5,7; Exod 19:18; 33:9; Num 11:17). When Jacob had a vision of God at Bethel, he called the place "the gate of heaven" because God's visitation had made that holy site a point of contact between heaven and earth (Gen 28:17). Later, the Temple in Jerusalem and its altar were symbols and sites of regular commerce between heaven and earth (Isa 6; Hag 2:1–9).

Some passages in the Hebrew scriptures hesitate to speak of God leaving heaven for earth. They rather emphasize God's total and complete transcendence. The Book of Deuteronomy, for example, stresses that God always remains in heaven and that any divine-human contact is made by the power of the name of God or the word of God on human lips (Deut 12:11; 30:11–14). Other texts ascribe divine intervention to God's angel who is sent to earth to do God's bidding (Exod 23:20). God as God remains in heaven. This "distancing" was to emphasize God's holiness and to remind people that no place on earth could ever contain God. In fact, some texts remind us that neither the heavens nor even the "highest heavens" (the region above the firmament) can contain God, who is transcendent to all created reality (1 Kgs 8:27; 2 Chr 2:6; 6:18).

God's transcendence or holiness does not mean, however, that God is remote and unconcerned with human fate. God knows all things and rules over all creation (Jer 23:23–24; Ps 139:7–12). So heaven, as God's dwelling place, remains the source of our salvation and hope (Gen 49:25; Deut 33:13; 1 Kgs 8:35–36). Hebrew scriptures look ahead to the end of time when God will create a *new* heaven and a *new* earth (Isa 65:17; 66:22). In that new creation the just will enjoy salvation in communion with God (Ps 73:23–28).

82. Is heaven mentioned in the Christian New Testament?

As with so many ideas in the New Testament, the notion of heaven is received from the Hebrew scriptures and then understood in light of the early Christians' faith in Jesus. In the New Testament, heaven is the divine realm, as it was in the writings of the Hebrew ancestors. As such it is the "place" from which Jesus has come. Isaiah's plea that God "rend the heavens and come down" is fulfilled in Christ (Isa 64:1).

In John's Gospel, Jesus is the preexisting Word of God, dwelling with God before creation, who comes down from heaven to "pitch his tent among us," as the Greek text literally says (John 1:1–3,10–14). Jesus has come down from heaven and will return to the Father who sent him (John 3:13,17; 6:38,42,50; 16:28). The scene of the ascension of Jesus after his death and resurrection dramatizes this return of Jesus to the right hand of God the Father, that is, the place of honor and power in heaven (Mark 16:19; Luke 24:50–51; Acts 1:9–11; see also John 7:62; 20:17).

When Jesus comes again at the end of time in glory, it will be from heaven (Mark 13:26; 14:62; Matt 24:30). After the final judgment, Jesus will take the just with him back to heaven where they will live with him and the Father in glory (1 Thess 4:16–17; Rev 19).

The Book of Revelation, hearkening back to the prophet Isaiah (Isa 65:17; 66:22), proclaims that God will make a *new* heaven and a *new* earth at the end of time (Rev 21:1,5). The New Testament asserts that God's creative work is not yet finished (see also 2 Pet 3:13). All of reality, even heaven, will be transformed and fulfilled by a new creative act of God (Rom 8:19–22). That transformation and fulfillment, like the first creation, will happen in, through, and with Christ. In Christ all creation—including heaven—once came into being and forever continues in being (Col 1:15–17). Christ fills every part of heaven and earth (Eph 1:23). Through Christ all things will be renewed (Rev 21:5).

It is fair to say that in the Bible the notion of heaven is not just a static place or fixed state where the blessed go upon death. It is a dynamic reality full of divine, creative activity for the benefit of God's people and the completion of creation. In the New Testament all such divine presence and activity is focused and centered in the mystery of Christ who rules in heaven.

83. Is there a difference between heaven and the kingdom of God?

Yes, there is a difference. The kingdom of God is less about heaven and more about earth. This phrase "kingdom of God," or "reign of God" as it is sometimes translated, comes from Jewish apocalyptic literature. It refers to a future time or messianic age when the entire human family will acknowledge God, act according to God's will, and live in ways that promote justice and peace for all peoples. The kingdom of God is the main focus of Jesus' preaching. "Jesus came to Galilee, proclaiming the good news of

God, and saying, 'The time is fulfilled, and the kingdom of God has come near...'" (Mark 1:14–15; Matt 4:17; see also Mark 4:26; 9:1; 10:25). In a sense we could say that the kingdom of God is "heaven on earth," that is, it is the just and peaceful society that would result from all humanity believing and living as if God were among us.

While we often presume that Jesus was sent to prepare our souls for heaven, his preaching is more often about how to build a better Earth. Christians may have heaven as their final destination, but the way to divine glory is through the building of an ever more just and humane world here and now. That is the kingdom of God.

In the actual texts of the Gospels, Matthew very often uses the phrase "kingdom of heaven" instead of the phrase "kingdom of God." Matthew's expression "kingdom of heaven" refers to the effects of God's grace and power among human beings on this Earth, especially as exemplified in the Christian community.

Heaven refers to the dwelling place of God and of Christ, where the just will share in eternal glory. The *kingdom of God* is more the expression of an ideal human society. Yet despite this difference in meaning, the two concepts are related. It is only by God's dwelling among us and by our living in God through Christ and the Holy Spirit that humanity will ever be able to achieve the kingdom of God. Conversely, the ideal society envisioned in the phrase "kingdom of God" may somehow lead to, prepare us for, or even help effect our participation in and experience of the reality of heaven.

Catholic Teaching about Heaven

84. What does the church teach about heaven?

Heaven is the state of full and everlasting communion with the Holy Trinity—God Creator (Father), Redeemer (Son), and Sanctifier (Holy Spirit). It is a state of perfect joy and happiness because we will have reached the true purpose and only satisfying goal of our existence: loving union with our God. It is the fulfillment of all our longings, the completion of our being, the realization of our deepest capacities for surrender, ecstasy, and intimacy in a full and immediate knowing and loving the very Source of being. (See the *Catechism of the Catholic Church,* pars. 1023–1029.)

Heaven is our inclusion in the inner life of the Trinity. Our union with Christ, begun in baptism, will be fulfilled as Christ brings us into his loving and being loved by God the Father/Mother/Creator. We will be immersed in and transformed by the Holy Spirit who is the living reality of the love between Father and Son, between the Creator and the eternal Word. Heaven is being completely and fully loved by the Source of love.

Heaven is also our full and irrevocable acceptance of this divine self-giving. Our acceptance of God's invitation is made possible only because the divine love itself transforms our being and infinitely expands our capacity to know and love. It is by God's grace that we become capable of eternal life and love. Heaven as such is the destiny of all, because in assuming our human nature Christ has made it possible for all people to enter into the life of God.

85. Isn't heaven a physical place like the scenes depicted in religious art?

No, heaven is not a place; it is a relationship. Heaven is our relationship with the Holy Trinity made possible by our union with Christ. Over the centuries, Christian artists have used such artistic effects as light, sky colors, clouds, and winged and singing angels to express the many dimensions of heavenly union with God. Artists, architects, musicians, and sculptors have stretched, deepened, and extended their talents to capture some semblance of divine glory, transcendence, happiness, and communion among the saints and angels. The beauty and symbolic power of religious and liturgical art, however, are meant to lift our minds and hearts to the possibility and meaning of union with God rather than to provide reliable descriptions of a physical place.

This is not to say that heaven is solely a disembodied spiritual state, over and against physical creation. The scriptural teachings of the resurrection of Christ and the resurrection of the body at the end of time, and the Catholic teaching of Mary's assumption into heaven, body and soul, at her death (question 90) all point to heaven as a state of union with God that somehow includes a transformed physical creation, the "new heaven and new earth" mentioned in Revelation 21:1.

So heaven is not a place to which our souls go upon death. It is a new kind of existence in God that transforms our being and all being. Religious art can be understood to be inspired by and in some way anticipate and even participate in that transformation of all creation.

86. Will I go to heaven right after I die?

Since the proclamation of *Benedictus Deus* by Pope Benedict XII in 1336, the church has formally taught that all persons who die in the state of grace enter immediately into heaven and do not have to wait until the return of Christ, the end of time, and the last judgment. The only delay to immediate union with God would be unresolved issues from sinful acts or intentions that might require a "time" of purgation (questions 37, 38, 39).

87. Will all people who have lived good lives go to heaven?

It is Catholic teaching that union with God is made possible for all human beings through, with, and in Christ (see the *Catechism of the Catholic Church,* pars. 1058–1060, 1260). Even all those who preceded Jesus in history and those who have never heard the gospel have access to God through Christ by virtue of their own human nature. In Christ God assumed and transformed our human nature. When a good-living woman or man struggles with the questions of human existence, strives to live with respect for others, and remains open to the dignity of human love, her or his own life journey becomes a pilgrimage of hope and love. As they enter ever more deeply into the mystery of their own humanity, they enter into the mystery of God who assumed that humanity in Christ.

In Catholic teaching the incarnation of the Word—the Son of God becoming human—has made a sacrament of all humanity. Through Christ all of creation is filled with the Holy Spirit (Joel 3:1–2; Isa 44:3; Acts 2:17–21). Christian faith sheds light on this mystery of God's offering of universal salvation, celebrates it, and announces the hope it inspires.

The Risen Body

88. What will my risen body be like?

This question is as old as Christianity itself. The Christians in Corinth asked Paul about the nature of the resurrected body. He answered with the metaphor of seed and plant: "And as for what you sow, you do not sow the body that is to be, but a bare seed, perhaps of wheat or of some other grain. But God gives it a body as he has chosen, and to each kind of seed its own body....So it is with the resurrection of the dead. What is sown is perishable, what is raised is imperishable. It is sown in dishonor, it is raised in glory. It is sown in weakness, it is raised in power. It is sown a physical body, it is raised a spiritual body" (1 Cor 15:37–38, 42–44).

This metaphor emphasizes differences between the physical body that is the seat of our existence in this life, and the spiritual body that will be the center of our eternal communion with God. They are as different as a flat, dry little seed and the tall, luscious, flowering plant it eventually produces. Yet the metaphor also allows for continuity. Only this seed will produce that kind of plant. Whatever the change in my being entailed by the resurrection of the body, there will be continuity between who I am now and who I will be in heaven (question 22). This change, which Paul says will happen "in a moment, in the twinkling of an eye" at the end of time (1 Cor 15:52), will not be the annihilation of the body, but its transformation.

Throughout Christian history, many have speculated on the qualities and characteristics of the risen, spiritual body, on what it will be capable of and how it may navigate space and perceive the universe. The 1979 "Letter on Certain Questions Concerning Eschatology" published by the Vatican's Sacred Congregation for the Doctrine of the Faith discouraged such speculation and urged Christians to stay closer to what scripture says about the afterlife, even if it is rather limited with regard to such details.

89. But will my body be the same physical matter that it is now?

We don't know. Remember, however, that the continuity of person or of our sense of self, even in this life, does not depend only on our physical bodies. Our life experiences, our memories, and our hopes all fashion who we are and how we experience ourselves (question 23). Certainly our mental or spiritual life resides in and depends on our body and brain. But consider that the body itself is constantly shedding, transforming, and creating new molecules, cells, and structures. Our memories are experienced in mysterious electrochemical flashes and patterns that we have hardly begun to understand. Our embodied existence in this life is a continual dance between matter and energy and our environment, and the elusive, inscrutable spaces among them. The multilayered questions and shifting paradigms of science provide much to consider regarding the nature of human sensation, thought, feeling, and choice.

Our experience of all creation is received, mediated, and interpreted through our bodily existence in this life. The resurrection of the body affirms that our communion with God in heaven will include a continued knowledge and love of all creation via new ways that are somehow continuous with our earthly existence and at the same time transformed by our sharing in the life of the Trinity.

90. If Jesus and Mary already have risen bodies in heaven, how are they different from everyone else in heaven before the final resurrection?

The teaching that Jesus rose from the dead and ascended into heaven affirms that his full humanity—body and soul—is in communion with Father and the Spirit. Jesus is "the beginning, the firstborn of the dead" (Col 1:18) in that the transformation and renewal of all creation has already begun through, with, and in the risen humanity of Christ.

The Catholic Church has a long tradition of believing that upon her death Mary, the mother of Jesus, shared in the resurrection of her son in such a way that her humanity was totally transformed—body and soul—and so anticipates the renewal of the rest of creation at the end of time. This teaching, called "the Assumption of Mary into Heaven," was promulgated as an official dogma of the church by Pius XII on November 1, 1950.

So Catholic teaching is that in the risen Jesus and the glorified mother of God, the restoration, fulfillment, and glorification of all creation is anticipated and promised. The blessed in heaven are different from Jesus and Mary in the sense that their union with God has yet to be completed by the resurrection of the body and the final renewal of all creation—the "new heaven and new earth" of Revelation 21:1. However, in this discussion we must remember that our category of time may not apply in neat and corresponding ways to the mysteries of eternity (question 21).

91. What age will I be in heaven?

Here again we are using a category of time, namely the passing of years, to inquire about eternity. It is pure speculation to set a "perfect" age that people will be in heaven. Rather, if we use the

categories of transformation and renewal that we find in scripture
(1 Cor 15), we could say that no matter how old or young we are
at the time of our death, our humanity will be recreated and
renewed by God's infinite love and grace. A weak parallel would
be how even human love can transform and renew the beloved at
any age.

92. Will people who have suffered from mental illness, physical disabilities, or mental retardation enjoy full mental health and capacity in heaven?

The transformation and renewal by divine grace and love
that attend our entrance into heavenly glory will restore, heal, and
invigorate our humanity. All human illness and suffering will be
done away with.

Consider that the miracles of Jesus addressed human illness,
suffering, and debility. In Jesus' miracles we have the beginning, the
first glimpse, of the new creation as experienced by individuals who
encountered Jesus on this Earth and professed faith in him. At the
end of time that same divine creative power that emerged in and
through Jesus' miracles will heal and make whole all of creation.

Over the centuries, whenever the church recognizes miracles of healing or restoration, it affirms them as incursions of
divine power that heal and restore in anticipation of the "new
heaven and new earth" that are part of the divine plan for all creation (Rev 21:1,5). Both Christ's healing ministry during his life
on Earth and the occasional miracles recognized by the church
provide assurance that all the blessed in heaven will also enjoy the
wholeness and perfection of their humanity.

93. Will infants, children, even fetuses be full human beings once they reach heaven?

Even a moment's thought of the vast numbers of infants,
children, and unborn who have met premature and untimely death
throughout human history can be overwhelming. The ravages of

disease, natural disasters, war, and abortion take a special toll on the weak and defenseless. In the Hebrew scriptures God speaks of special concern about such members of the human family and constantly upbraids his people and their leaders for not protecting and defending the poor and powerless (Isa 1–3; Jer 2). It would seem a fair conclusion of Christian faith that God will provide for those whose human life and experience in this world were elementary or even preliminary.

Jesus showed special regard for children. "Let the little children come to me, and do not stop them; for it is to such as these that the kingdom of heaven belongs" (Matt 19:14; see also Matt 18:2–4; Mark 10:14–16). Luke's Gospel notes that Jesus wanted babies to have free access to his blessing (Luke 18:15–17). God must have some provision for their share as full and perfected human beings in the transformation and renewal of all creation and in the joy of heaven (questions 49, 50).

The Communion of Saints

94. Will there be a sense of community and shared life in heaven?

The teaching of the communion of saints affirms a loving relationship among all those who are united in Christ. The faithful on Earth, souls in purgatory, and the blessed in heaven are all members of the mystical body of Christ, all united with God by the power of the Holy Spirit. This is one of the oldest Christian doctrines found in the ancient creeds.

This doctrine of the communion of saints also reflects the many passages of scripture that refer to heaven as a community of love whose members are united in God. Jesus uses the image of the wedding banquet to speak about the kingdom of God (Matt 22:1–13; Luke 14:16–24). It is an image of joy and happiness among participants who are celebrating the closest of human relationships. Jesus promises the good thief that "today you will be with me in paradise" (Luke 23:42), proclaiming from the cross that heaven is relationship with him. Paul assures the Thessalonians that they will be reunited with their departed loved ones, and then united with them and Christ (1 Thess 4:17). Love will never fail; it will last forever (1 Cor 13:8,13). Nothing, not even death, can separate us from the love of Christ (Rom 8:38–39).

Saint John tells us that "God is love, and those who abide in love abide in God, and God abides in them" (1 John 4:16). This love will be perfected in heaven (1 John 4:17–18). What the fullness of love and community will be like in heaven we cannot yet know. John writes, however, that our experience of the loving community of heaven will involve our immediate experience of God and of each other in God (1 John 3:2).

95. Will all persons of every faith or of no faith be together in heaven?

The distinctions and separations among world religions will not apply in heaven. Such differences are the result of history, culture, language, philosophy, theology, and social structures. With the end of history and the creation of a "new heaven and new earth" (Rev 21:1), all the just will be united with God and with each other in the eternal, loving life of the Holy Trinity. Christians believe that this final transformation and salvation will happen through Christ in whom humanity and divinity are reconciled and united (*Catechism of the Catholic Church,* par. 2550).

96. Will my family, my spouse, or my children be more important to me than other people in heaven?

Yes, in a way. Christian teaching values the individual and her or his identity and memory (questions 22, 23). So those who have been part of our earthly lives will be part of our experience in the community of the blessed in heaven. We will, however, know, understand, value, and love them in a new way, transformed by our common share in the life of the Trinity. Jesus' admonition that "in the resurrection they neither marry nor are given in marriage, but are like angels in heaven" (Matt 22:30) signals that our way of relating will be different. In the new creation all our relationships will be recreated and perfected. Yet those who have been dear to us in this life will be so in the next. Jesus says as much during his last talk with his own friends: "And if I go and prepare a place for you, I will come again and will take you to myself, so that where I am, there you may be also" (John 14:3).

There is a related question: What about family members or friends who may reject God and be in hell? Wouldn't their situation sadden us? In response to this question theologians have simply affirmed that nothing can detract from or threaten the happiness of heaven. The failure of loved ones to share in the communion of saints will not distract us from the new life we enjoy in God.

97. Will there be some people in heaven who are more important, like priests or popes?

No. Such distinctions are also accidents of history, culture, and society. They will be eclipsed by the glory of heaven. The church has taught that those who have lived especially holy lives on Earth or who have suffered much in this life may have by virtue of such experience a greater capacity to receive divine love and so a greater degree of eternal happiness (Council of Florence, 1439). In that sense many good persons, though unknown and uncelebrated in religious or secular history, may enjoy a fuller experience of God. Such distinctions about "gradations of heavenly happiness," however, are rather ethereal theological speculation.

98. Will there really be angels in heaven like you see in religious pictures?

Christian teaching about angels comes from the Bible and from later theological reflection. Angels appear early in Hebrew scriptures. They are powerful, spiritual beings who, using the imagery of the period, were understood to attend God in the divine court of heaven (Gen 28:12; Job 1:6; 2:1; Ezek 1; Dan 3:55,58; 7:9–10). They also function as divine messengers, bringing God's Word to earth (Gen 16:7–12; 21:17–18) or executing God's will (Exod 14:19; 2 Kgs 19:35). The mention of angels increases in the later Hebrew books and in Jewish apocalyptic literature. They receive names like Gabriel (Dan 8:16) and Michael (Dan 12:1) and are assigned tasks in salvation history. By the time of Jesus, angels figure prominently as divinely appointed guardians, companions, and intercessors in the popular Jewish religion of that era.

The New Testament authors assume the existence of angels and incorporate them into their major themes. Gabriel announces to Mary her divinely appointed mission (Luke 1:26). Zechariah (Luke 1:11), Joseph (Matt 1:20; 2:19), and the shepherds of Bethlehem (Luke 2:8–15) are all visited by angels. They minister to Jesus after his temptation in the desert (Matt 4:11) and in Gethsemane (Luke 22:43). Jesus speaks of little children having guardian angels (Matt 18:10). The apostles are helped by angels in their ministry (Acts 12:7–15). Angels populate the Book of Revelation, where they worship God in heaven (Rev 4; 8:3–5) and carry out God's will both in heaven and on earth (Rev 8:6–13; 9; 10; 14; 15; 16).

The church has taught the existence of angels as incorporeal creatures who, like human beings, are called into relationship with God through Christ, the divine Word through whom all things—including angels—were created (Lateran Council IV in 1215, Vatican Council I from 1869 to 1870). Over the centuries there has been much (and sometimes quite inventive) theological speculation about the nature and number of angels. Beyond affirming their existence and their submission to Christ (Mark 13:32; Gal 1:8; Col 1:16; 2:18; Heb 1:4), official church teaching says little about them.

The scriptural scenes in Daniel and Revelation that describe angels ministering to and worshiping God in heaven began quite early to influence how Christians understood their own liturgical worship. Just as angels were thought to attend worship in the Temple in Jerusalem (Isa 6:1–7), Christians believed angels were present worshiping with them at the celebration of Eucharist (1 Cor 11:10). This belief influenced liturgical art so that angels are often depicted in mosaics, frescoes, and paintings as worshiping together with the Christian assembly.

So angels are expected in Christian faith to be part of the experience of our communion with God and each other in heaven.

99. Will we be able to relate to angels in heaven?

The essence of heaven, as we have said (question 84), is relationship with the Holy Trinity through our incorporation into Christ. According to Christian teaching about angels, they, too, are part of the life in God through Christ. We don't often think of angels as needing Christ's redemptive work; and since they are incorporeal, they certainly aren't baptized. Yet all creation, including angels, came into being through the Word of God (John 1:1–3). As creatures, angels are also part of the renewal and transformation of all creation in and through Christ (Rev 21:5). So we share with the angels our life with God through Christ.

The traditional teaching about angels is that they, like us, are intelligent beings capable of choice. Their inclusion in heaven is the result of their response to the eternal invitation of divine love.

It can be instructive, and even perhaps disconcerting, to think about heaven as including creatures other than human who also share in the life of the Holy Trinity. Yet at this point in human history, when the vastness of the universe and the possibilities of multiple forms of intelligent life beyond our galaxy challenge our assumptions, the ancient tradition of angels can keep our minds and hearts open. Angels, understood as incorporeal beings, intelligent and capable of love, are not uninvolved in the material universe. Scripture and Christian tradition accepts their existence and their active partnership with God and with the human family in the building of society and the work of salvation.

In the Middle Ages angels functioned to help philosophers and theologians provide metaphysical examples of finite, nonmaterial, intellectual beings. Perhaps they can help us citizens of the twenty-first century reflect on how God's infinite love extends throughout the physical universe in ways we can hardly imagine. The possibility of being able to relate in heaven with these spiritual, loving beings is perhaps a glimpse of "what God has prepared for those who love him" (1 Cor 2:9).

100. What does "beatific vision" mean?

Medieval theologians asked the basic question: How can created, finite beings such as humans or angels possibly have a relationship with the infinite, eternal being that is God? There is just too much difference between them. An analogous question would be: How could a life form that lacks human intelligence and love, like a mouse, ever relate on the same level with a human being? The theological answer, debated and developed over centuries of Christian thought, is that left to our own natural capacities and resources, we could never entertain an immediate, face-to-face relationship with God. All we have—even with Christian faith—are ideas *about* God, mediated by and through human language that employs analogies, comparisons, and symbols when attempting to speak about God and ultimate matters (see the Introduction to this volume, pages 1–5).

There are many passages in scripture that reflect on this theme. When Moses asks to see God's face, the Lord responds, "You cannot see my face; for no one shall see me and live" (Exod 33:20). John echoes this theme in the very first chapter of his Gospel: "No one has ever seen God" (John 1:18; see also 5:37; 6:46; 2 Cor 5:7).

Yet we have the desire for an immediate, everlasting relationship with God. Indeed, *only* such relationship with God will ever fully and finally meet the profound human quest for meaning, purpose, and happiness. Saint Augustine expressed this in the famous words at the beginning of his *Confessions:* "You have made us for yourself, O Lord, and our hearts are restless until they rest in You" (Bk. I, Chap. I).

Christ answers this deepest of all human needs. Jesus reveals to us the nature, the "face of God." "Whoever has seen me has seen the Father" (John 14:9; see also 8:19; 10:30,38; 12:45). Jesus also gives us the gift of the Holy Spirit, which renews and transforms our humanity to make it capable of and adequate to a "face-to-face" relationship with God (John 16:13; Rom 8:9–11,14–17).

In baptism we are already drawn into the mystery of Christ by the power of the Holy Spirit. At death the fullness of our life in Christ is revealed to us and we enter into "face-to-face" relationship with the Holy Trinity. The beatific vision is a "seeing" that will make us "happy" (*beatify* means "to make happy"). Faith and theology, which rely on analogy and mediated knowledge, will be replaced by an immediate, intuitive knowing and loving of God. As Saint Paul wrote, "For now we see in a mirror, dimly, but then we will see face to face. Now I know only in part; then I will know fully, even as I have been fully known" (1 Cor 13:12).

EPILOGUE

...but then we will see face to face.
— 1 Corinthians 13:12

101. So what might these questions and answers mean for how I live my life?

In the end all of us—believers or not—must surrender to the mystery that is death. To surrender is to put oneself in the hands of another, to give up power and advantage, to forego control. Surrender may be to an enemy who assumes power over us. In such cases *surrender* means defeat. Death can seem like an enemy, stalking us all our life long, waiting silently in the shadows for the chance to annihilate us. Surrendering to such an inevitable enemy may appear to be our final defeat.

Yet we also speak of surrender to a loved one, putting ourselves in the hands of someone we cherish, someone with whom we are willing to entrust our very lives. Such surrender is a victory of and for love. Christian teachings about the four last things show us that death is more like the act of surrendering in love. Our very last human act is an opportunity to put ourselves completely in the hands of Christ, to give him all power and control, to let go and trust that our dying is finally a sharing in the loving victory of Christ over death.

Some people die like Jesus on the cross, consciously surrendering themselves into the Father's good hands (Luke 23:46). Medical personnel will tell you how they have watched as many elderly persons, after long and loving lives, spend their last hours taking leave of children, grandchildren, and great grandchildren, thanking each of them for being a part of their lives. Then they close their eyes and die, as if by simply willing it. Such surrender is the gracious final act of a graciously lived life.

For others death is quick and unexpected, by accident or malicious intent. For many, pain, mental or physical, may be their final companion, distracting them from all else. Yet, even in such cases, is not death by its very nature the surrendering of life? The act of dying, be it with full awareness and intent, be it unbidden or unconscious, be it sudden or slow, means relinquishing power and control, facing the unknown, separating from the security of our human being as we know it.

Surrender, however, can be an attitude and an act that characterizes our entire Christian life. By baptism we are already incorporated into the risen Christ. We have, in a very real sense, already surrendered our lives to him. In prayer and meditation we can surrender to Christ each day, acknowledging the presence and power of the Holy Spirit in our lives, allowing ourselves to be guided and prompted by divine love in our daily dealings and decisions. Christian teachings about the four last things can instruct us in the habit of surrender to God by encouraging our prayerful meditation on what our ancestors in the faith have said about ultimate matters. If we have developed the spiritual virtue of surrender over a lifetime, our final surrender in faith and hope at the end becomes an ultimate act of loving trust in the God who has guided us in this world and who will receive us lovingly into the next.

GLOSSARY OF TERMS

Apocalypse Another name for the last book of the New Testament, also called the Book of Revelation or simply Revelation. It comes from the Greek word *apokalyptein,* meaning "to uncover" or "to reveal." The Apocalypse or Revelation is the longest and greatest example of Christian apocalyptic literature.

apocalyptic literature A distinct kind of literature that followed and developed out of the prophetic movement in Judaism during the Babylonian exile (587–38 BCE) and the following five centuries. It emphasized God's power and action in the world to overcome evil despots and empires. It is characterized by exuberant and fantastic symbolism, often difficult to understand, and by a belief in angels and in the resurrection of the dead. Jewish apocalyptic writings were popular during the time of Jesus and influenced his preaching and the faith of the early Christian communities. The main apocalyptic writings in the Hebrew Bible are Ezekiel and Daniel, and in the New Testament the Book of Revelation. There are also apocalyptic passages in the Gospels (Mark 13, Matt 24, Luke 21) and in some New Testament letters (for example, 1 Thess 4:13–5:11; 2 Pet 3).

Bible The sacred books of the Jews and Christians. The Hebrew Bible (also called the "Hebrew scriptures" or "Old Testament") contains forty-six books, according to Catholics, and thirty-nine books according to Jews and Protestants. The seven disputed books, called "deuterocanonical" or "apocryphal," are the result of disagreements between rabbis in Alexandria, Egypt (who considered forty-six books acceptable), and rabbis in Palestine (who accepted only thirty-nine). The New Testament contains twenty-seven books, including the four Gospels, the Acts of the Apostles, twenty-one letters, and Revelation.

church The community of believing Christians who profess faith in Jesus Christ as lord and savior. The three main kinds of Christian churches are Roman Catholic, Protestant, and Orthodox, which share a common faith in Jesus and in baptism in his name, but which define, explain, and ritually celebrate that same faith in different ways developed over centuries of tradition, teaching, and worship.

church council A meeting of church leaders, usually bishops and archbishops who, assisted by theologians, deliberate on important questions of faith or morals; councils can be local gatherings of the bishops of a region, or global, ecumenical meetings of bishops from around the world under the leadership of the pope.

communion of saints The Christian teaching, found in ancient creeds or professions of faith, that all believers in Christ—those on Earth, those in purgatory, and those in heaven—are mystically united with each other in Christ by the power of the Holy Spirit.

creed A formal statement or profession of faith that expresses the most important beliefs or teachings of the church. The early creeds resulted from the deliberation and reflection of church councils.

death The cessation of life; death can be defined clinically, biologically, philosophically, or theologically. Theologically, death has been understood as the separation of body and soul and as the return of the soul to the Creator for judgment.

eschatology From the Greek word *eschaton,* which means "end"; it is the careful, theological reflection on the meaning of life and of the universe in light of the ends or purposes for which God created all things.

Fathers of the Church The leading Christian thinkers and writers from the second to the seventh or eighth century who helped form Christian teaching and practice in light of the Bible and of philosophical schools of their day. The patriarchal nature of society at that time precluded women from recognition as theological writers.

gospel From an Old English word meaning "good news," "story," or "message"; in Greek *euvangelion* has the same meaning. In the New Testament there are four Gospels: the three Synoptic Gospels of Matthew, Mark, and Luke, and the differently styled Gospel of John.

heaven The final state of glory and happiness in which the just and the angels share completely and forever in the life of the Holy Trinity. Heaven is also understood as the "abode" of God.

hell The final state of the unjust and the devils who have rejected God's offer of love and forgiveness and who therefore exist forever separated from God.

Hebrew scriptures Also called the "Hebrew Bible," and by Christians the "Old Testament'; thirty-nine books that reflect and express the faith experience of the early Hebrew descendants of Abraham and Sarah (around 1800 BCE) as it developed under the leadership of Moses (around 1250 BCE), the kings, and prophets (around 1000 to 500 BCE), and the religion called "Judaism" that emerged after the Babylonian exile (587–38 BCE). There were seven additional books, called "deuterocanonical" or "apocryphal," accepted as inspired by the rabbis in Alexandria, Egypt, but not by the rabbis in Palestine.

Holy Spirit The "third person" of the Holy Trinity, understood to be the gift of Jesus to his followers and the animating principle of the church, as well as the divine presence permeating all of creation.

Holy Trinity The Christian doctrine that there are three persons in one God: Father (Creator), Son (Redeemer or Word), and Holy Spirit (Sanctifier). Christians do not teach that there are three gods, but three distinct yet interpenetrating dimensions of the mystery of the Holy One. This mystery was prefigured in Hebrew scriptures but revealed by Christ who always referred to God as Father and who promised the Holy Spirit. Christians believe that heaven is a state of sharing fully, body and soul, in the loving communion among these three divine persons.

judgment In the biblically based religions of Judaism, Christianity, and Islam, the belief that all persons are held accountable for their intentions, decisions, and actions. In Christianity, Christ is understood to be the judge of all humankind. The Hebrew understanding of *judge,* carried over into the New Testament, is one who liberates and empowers as well as one who holds transgressors accountable.

New Testament The twenty-seven books, including the four Gospels, the Acts of the Apostles, twenty-one letters, and Revelation, considered by all Christian churches to be inspired by the Holy Spirit and authentic proclamations of the meaning of Jesus' preaching, miracles, and identity as the Son of God and savior. The New Testament authors either witnessed the life and preaching of Jesus themselves or knew those who did.

Old Testament See **Hebrew scriptures.**

prophet A holy man or woman in the Hebrew scriptures who interpreted the meaning of events in the life of God's people in light of God's law and will. Often prophets challenged Jewish leaders to return to observance of the Torah or Law and its teachings of justice. Prophets emerged as the institution of kingship emerged (around 1000 BCE), grew in importance in the eighth and seventh centuries, and lasted until the Babylonian exile (587–38 BCE).

prophetic literature The preaching and messages of the prophets preserved in the Hebrew scriptures, called *nebiim* in Hebrew and equal in importance to the Law (Torah) and the writings *(kethuvim)*. Early prophetic writings appear in books of Samuel and Kings. The period of classical Hebrew prophecy (eighth to sixth centuries) included Isaiah, Jeremiah, Ezekiel, and Hosea and twelve shorter books of so-called minor prophets.

resurrection of the body Christian belief that at the end of time and history all persons will be reunited with their physical body to enjoy the fullness of God and all of creation.

Revelation, Book of See **Apocalypse.**

sacrament A ritual symbol or action in Christian tradition that expresses an essential mystery of faith and through that expression invites participants into the grace of the same mystery. The Catholic Church celebrates seven sacraments: baptism, confirmation, Holy Eucharist, reconciliation, anointing of the sick, ordination, and marriage.

synod From the Greek word *synodos,* which means "gathering"; a synod is similar to a church council; the word is also used for a local or regional council. However, popes have also called worldwide meetings of bishops and laity that have been referred to as "synods." Generally in the Catholic Church, the term *council* implies a gathering to consider doctrinal or moral issues, while a synod may focus on specific pastoral questions or concerns. See also **church council.**

Synoptic Gospels The three Gospels of Matthew, Mark, and Luke. *Synoptic* (Greek meaning "looked at together") refers to the fact that when you put these three Gospels alongside each other, you can see that they share a similar overall structure, and in many places depend on each other and perhaps a common source in their proclamation of the life, preaching, and ministry of Jesus. However, these three Gospels also have differences in theological themes, literary style, and detail.

theology The classical definition of *theology* is "faith seeking understanding." It is a disciplined investigation of the mysteries and teachings of the faith shared by a community of believers. Theologians study the Bible, human reason, different schools of philosophy, and other academic disciplines to achieve deeper understandings of the meaning and implication of particular teachings of faith.

FOR FURTHER READING

Official Church Teachings and Statements

Catechism of the Catholic Church. United States Conference of Catholic Bishops, 1994. See pars. 631–67 (Christ's death, resurrection, and ascension); 668–82 (judgment); 988–1019 (resurrection); 1020–60 (judgment, heaven, purgatory, hell, eternal life); 1250–71 (sacrament of baptism). The entire Catechism is available online at *www.usccb.org*.

John Paul II. Text of papal audience on Wednesday, July 28, 1999. Available at *www.vatican.va,* the Holy Father, John Paul II, audiences, 1999.

Sacred Congregation for the Doctrine of the Faith. "Letter on Certain Questions Concerning Eschatology." 1979. Available at *www.catholicculture.org/index.cfm.* See also *www.vatican. va,* Roman Curia, Congregations, Doctrine of the Faith (doctrinal documents).

Death and Resurrection

Donovan, Jean. *The Mystery of Death: Reflections on the Spiritual Tradition.* Mahwah/New York: Paulist Press, 2003.

Perry, John Michael. *Exploring the Resurrection of Jesus.* Lanham: Sheed & Ward, 1993.

Segal, Alan. *Life after Death: A History of the Afterlife in Western Religion.* New York: Doubleday, 2004.

Wilson, Colin. *Afterlife: An Investigation.* New York: Doubleday, 1987.

Eschatology, End of Time

Bellitto, Christopher. *What Every Catholic Should Know about the Millennium.* Liguori: Liguori Publications, 1998.

Brown, Raymond; Kasper, Walter; O'Collins, Gerald; and Gavin, John. *Faith and the Future: Studies in Christian Eschatology.* Mahwah/New York: Paulist Press, 1994.

Hayes, Zachary. *Visions of a Future: A Study of Christian Eschatology—New Theology Series,* Vol. 8. Wilmington: Michael Glazier Books, 1992.

Hayes, Zachary. *What Are They Saying about the End of the World?* Mahwah/New York: Paulist Press, 1983.

Peters, Tiemo Rainer; and Urban, Claus, eds. *The End of Time? The Provocation of Talking about God.* Mahwah/New York: Paulist Press, 2004.

Stackhouse, Reginald. *The End of the World? A New Look at an Old Belief.* Mahwah/New York: Paulist Press, 1997.

Apocalyptic Literature

Faley, Roland. *Apocalyptic Then and Now: A Companion to the Book of Revelation.* Mahwah/New York: Paulist Press, 1999.

Lewis, Scott. *What Are They Saying about New Testament Apocalyptic?* Mahwah/New York: Paulist Press, 2003.

Ralph, Margaret Nutting. *The Bible and the End of the World: Should We Be Afraid?* Mahwah/New York: Paulist Press, 1997.

SCRIPTURE INDEX

Heaven

GENERAL INDEX

RESPONSES TO 101 QUESTIONS ABOUT JESUS
by Michael L. Cook, SJ

RESPONSES TO 101 QUESTIONS ON THE PSALMS
AND OTHER WRITINGS
by Roland E. Murphy, O Carm

RESPONSES TO 101 QUESTIONS ON DEATH AND
ETERNAL LIFE
by Peter C. Phan

RESPONSES TO 101 QUESTIONS ON HINDUISM
by John Renard

RESPONSES TO 101 QUESTIONS ON BUDDHISM
by John Renard

RESPONSES TO 101 QUESTIONS ON THE MASS
by Kevin W. Irwin

RESPONSES TO 101 QUESTIONS ON GOD AND EVOLUTION
by John F. Haught

RESPONSES TO 101 QUESTIONS ON
CATHOLIC SOCIAL TEACHING
by Kenneth R. Himes, OFM